COLLECTION STORIES

national museum of australia

DIRECTOR'S FOREWORD

The National Museum of Australia is the place where our stories live and where they *come to life*. This dual meaning goes to the distinctive quality of museums as institutions where stories are embodied in objects. Artefacts, material evidence, visual records — these are the mediums by which the past may be evoked, understood, interpreted and reinterpreted.

It was not an easy task to arrive at a selection of objects that covers the depth and range of the Museum's collection. Yet the objects included in this book do capture the *character* of the Museum. No matter how directed the collecting activity undertaken by museums, there will always be the accidental, the fortuitous or the downright quirky circumstances that lead to a collection having a particular shape and texture. Such is the history of the early development of the Museum's collection, outlined in Kirsten Wehner's introductory essay. Without understanding some of this history, it is not possible to understand the unique shape of our collection.

The Museum's collection encompasses the almost 60,000-year-old history of human occupation of the continent. Against this awesome timespan, the Museum's collection development has a relatively short history and involves rigorous processes to establish significance. Creating a collection of significant objects is quite a responsibility, one that the Museum's staff and Council take seriously. The breadth of the Museum's interests over time, the expertise and knowledge of curators, and the accidents of history, have created the multifarious and wide-ranging collection sampled in this book.

One remarkable quality of museum collections is the way in which they constantly yield new dimensions — in effect, new stories — as outcomes of research. Equally noteworthy is the way they acquire new facets of importance as a result of changing community interests and enthusiasm. It is therefore incumbent on museums to look after their collections for the future and to make them as widely accessible as possible. These things require both physical infrastructure and staff expertise, and much of the work of museums is devoted to these often costly and 'behind-the-scenes' responsibilities.

What do people expect of their National Museum? There are many answers to this question. Yet one common expectation is that an encounter with the Museum, be it as the result of a visit, an online interaction or through a book such as this, will yield some new insights into Australian history, creativity and ideas. I hope *Collection Stories* will give readers a new dimension of understanding, not only about the Museum, but also Australia itself.

Andrew Sayers
Director

COLLECTION
STORIES

At the heart of the National Museum of Australia sits the National Historical Collection, more than 210,000 objects representing the breadth and depth of life in Australia. It is an eclectic mix of items, incorporating objects of all shapes, sizes and materials. Some objects are big, some tiny and intimate. Some, such as the glass spear points made by Aboriginal people from the Kimberley in Western Australia, incorporate techniques of manufacture developed over thousands of years. Others, for example the Australian flag recovered from the ruins of the World Trade Center after it was destroyed on 11 September 2001, record terrible events of our recent history. Some items evoke the lives of well-known Australians, while others no less importantly illuminate the experiences of everyday people.

This book presents a small selection of the National Historical Collection's most significant and intriguing objects. Each tells a story, or many possible stories, about Australia's diverse peoples, environments and histories. They lead us into the lives of others, inviting us to imagine what the world was like when Burke and Wills perished after crossing the continent from south to north, leaving behind a worn leather water bottle, or when Pintupi artist Uta Uta Tjangala sat with men from his community painting *Yumari* and talking about ending their exile from their country. Individually, these objects connect us with others' experiences and perspectives on the world. Together, they reflect to us the complex, shifting shape of the Australian nation, inspiring us to explore who we are, where we've come from and how we might create our future.

First acquisitions

People often think of the National Museum of Australia as a young institution, in part because its public face — its major exhibitions and programs facility on Acton Peninsula in Canberra — was only opened in 2001 to celebrate Australia's Centenary of Federation. The National Historical Collection, however, has been developing over a much longer period. The Australian Government created the Museum in 1980 and, soon after, a range of material was transferred to the institution from other government agencies such as the Australian Institute of Anatomy, the Australian Institute of Aboriginal Studies (now the Australian Institute of Aboriginal and Torres Strait Islander Studies), the Australian Broadcasting Commission, the Bureau of Mineral Resources and the departments of Home Affairs, Transport and the Capital Territory.

The Museum acquired some of its most important and well-known objects from these foundation collections. The heart of the racehorse Phar Lap was originally part of the Institute of Anatomy collection. Phar Lap, the darling of Depression-era Australia, died suddenly in 1932 in the United States, soon after winning the prestigious Agua Caliente handicap. Rumours quickly spread that the Australian challenger had been poisoned by the 'Yanks' and the horse's heart was removed and sent to the University of Sydney for analysis. The test results proved inconclusive but scientists, and soon the public, were amazed by the unusually large size of the organ. Phar Lap became a legend and his heart was preserved and displayed for many years at the Institute of Anatomy building in Canberra.

The Institute closed in the early 1980s and Phar Lap's heart, together with about 2000 other wet specimens (animal specimens stored in preserving fluid), came into the Museum's care. Sir Colin MacKenzie, a Melbourne orthopaedic surgeon and passionate advocate for the importance of comparative anatomy in treating human injury and disease, built this amazing record of Australia's native fauna over several decades from the 1900s. He collected some highly significant items, including the only known complete carcass of the now extinct thylacine, or Tasmanian tiger. Phar Lap's heart, however, remains the most recognisable item in this collection. Eighty years after the horse's death, his heart is the Museum object most sought out by visitors and is now on permanent display in the Museum's Landmarks gallery.

The Institute of Anatomy collections also included over 20,000 ethnographic items, an important record of Indigenous technology, society and cosmology collected by anthropologists such as Edmund Milne, Herbert Basedow and AR Radcliffe-Brown between the 1870s and the 1970s. This material was transferred to the Museum when the Institute closed, becoming the core of the Museum's highly significant collection of Aboriginal and Torres Strait Islander material. The Museum also has a range of archaeological material in its collections from the over 60,000 year history of Aboriginal and Torres Strait Islander peoples occupation of the continent and islands we now know as Australia.

Many of these objects were originally acquired by collectors who believed they were documenting, at best, the passing of Australian Aboriginal traditional ways of life and, at worst, the existence of Indigenous peoples doomed to extinction by contact with European civilisation. These collections are today a significant record of Indigenous history and culture and the Museum now works with Aboriginal and Torres Strait Islander peoples to enable communities across Australia to reconnect with these objects as important elements of their contemporary culture.

The Institute of Anatomy acquired and housed ethnographic items in part because for many years there was no other government institution capable of properly storing this material. From the early 1960s, for example, the institute took responsibility for caring for the extensive range of Indigenous cultural artefacts collected by field researchers working through the Australian Institute of Aboriginal Studies. The Museum acquired this material in the 1980s together with the Institute of Anatomy's older collections. The transfer included particularly significant and extensive holdings of Aboriginal artworks on bark from northern Australia, including a range of works by Yolngu artist Narritjin Maymuru, one of Australia's greatest painters, depicting his clan lands in eastern Arnhem Land.

Individual items transferred from other Australian Government departments soon joined the Museum's acquisitions from the Institute of Anatomy. In many cases, these objects had been held for many years in anticipation of them being eventually housed in a national museum. In July 1928, for example, Australian adventurer Francis Birtles arrived in Melbourne in his 14-horsepower Bean two-seater and declared to the crowd that the Bean Company was donating the vehicle to the Australian Government on the condition that it be placed in the 'Museum in Canberra'. The car certainly deserved the accolade, for Birtles had just completed an overland trek of over 26,000 kilometres from London to Australia, taking nine months to drive through Europe, across the deserts of the Middle East and over almost impassable mountain tracks in Asia.

Of course, there was not as yet any 'Museum in Canberra' and, for the next 40 years, Birtles' Bean car languished in a series of storage sheds in Canberra, gradually falling into disrepair. Then two employees of the Department of Transport rediscovered the vehicle and set about restoring it, displaying it occasionally at vintage car rallies and various museums. The car finally found a permanent home and expert care when the Museum was established. Museum staff embarked on 12 months of innovative and painstaking conservation work, returning the vehicle not to its factory condition but rather, as closely as possible, to the state in which it arrived in Melbourne in 1928.

Building the collection

Since its foundation in 1980, the Museum's aim has been to document and interpret three interrelated themes in Australia's past: Aboriginal and Torres Strait Islander cultures and histories, Australian history and society, and people's interaction with the environment. Together, these themes provide a framework for the National Historical Collection — they guide Museum curators in thinking and talking about the collection, and in finding and interpreting new material for the collection.

While these three themes provide what you might call the enduring skeleton of the National Historical Collection, each generation of curators also shapes the 'body' in different ways. Curators develop the collection in the context of the thematic framework but they also identify and select new acquisitions in response to the prevailing concerns and ideas of the day. Sir Colin MacKenzie developed the Museum's founding Institute of Anatomy collections because he believed that the comparative study of the 'simpler' anatomical forms of animals could provide insights into the human body. Today, comparative anatomy has fallen out of fashion, and Museum curators now tend to explore the Institute of Anatomy collections in terms of how they reveal past European–Australian attitudes to Australian fauna.

As the Museum established itself through the 1980s, the development of the National Historical Collection was strongly informed by the emergence of 'social history'. This movement argued, in contrast to the prevailing wisdom, that the lives of everyday people were as important in understanding historical change as the achievements of the important and powerful. At the Museum, curators embraced this insight by developing targeted collecting projects designed to build the National Historical Collection's material relating to working and domestic life, popular culture and leisure. The Museum acquired examples of objects such as the Hills Hoist rotary clothesline and Victa lawnmower that appeared in Australian backyards across the nation. In 1985, it bought from its manufacturer a pink Propert 'Trailaway' caravan, a fitting and rather endearing testament to the thousands of Australian families who took to the roads in the 1950s to see their country.

Social history directed attention to Australians whose experiences had often been left out of official accounts of the nation's development. The Museum became particularly interested in the histories of working people, women and Australians from non-English-speaking backgrounds, and staff developed a historical, rather than anthropological, focus on the lives of Indigenous Australians. During the 1980s and 1990s, curators worked with a range of organisations and individuals to identify material to build the National Historical Collection's holdings related to these groups. This led to the acquisition of a number of significant collections, including the Waterside Workers' Federation of Australia's banner depicting labour on the Sydney docks, and Aboriginal activist Faith Bandler's white gloves, worn as a sign of her respectability as she campaigned for the 'Yes' vote in the 1967 referendum to change the Australian Constitution and end its discrimination against Indigenous people.

During this period, the Museum completed a significant collecting project focusing on Australia's migrant heritage, reflecting its broader commitment to recording and interpreting the diversity of a multicultural nation. Over several years, curators developed relationships with people from many different areas of the world, including post-war migrants from across Europe and families who fled to Australia from South-East Asia. At a Melbourne conference in 1988, sociologist Professor Jerzy Zubrzycki, then a Museum consultant, met Mrs Guna Kinne, who had arrived in Australia in 1948 after fleeing the Soviet annexation of Latvia and the horrors of wartime Europe. During a casual conversation, Kinne told Zubrzycki about her national costume, an outfit of eight different pieces that she had made over a period of 20 years. It was one of the few possessions Kinne was able to take with her when she escaped the forces invading her homeland.

Kinne decided to donate her national costume to the Museum, 'putting aside', as she put it, 'an important banner from the past'. The donation proved, however, far from a one-time event. In 2006, Kinne gave the Museum the final element of her national costume, an amber necklace, representative of the significance of amber to Latvia, and the pattern book she used to make her costume. The following year, she donated items, including two of her paintings, reflecting her continued sense of connection to both the places of her Latvian childhood and her first home in Australia, on the Murray River in Victoria. Through these generous gifts, the Museum built up an important and moving record of one woman's life story and the broader history of how migration shaped Australia.

Objects and exhibitions

Museum curators develop the National Historical Collection in relation to the Museum's thematic framework and broader evolving understandings of history, but also in the context of producing exhibitions, one of the key ways in which the Museum communicates with audiences. In 1997, the Australian Government provided funding for the Museum to develop a major new exhibition and public program facility on Acton Peninsula in Canberra. Museum staff enthusiastically set to work developing exhibition concepts and stories, exploring existing material in the National Historical Collection and identifying areas for new acquisitions required to interpret the breadth of Australian history.

Some individual objects became the centrepiece of entire galleries. Inspired by a preacher encouraging him to contemplate the afterlife, Arthur Stace spent 35 years chalking the word 'Eternity' on Sydney's footpaths, walls and other surfaces. He remained anonymous for much of that time, his signs intriguing the city's residents as they encountered them each day. In the early 1960s, Stace wrote his word on a piece of black card and gave it to a friend, Thelma Dodds, who had often provided him with a meal when he was homeless and broke. Dodds later gave the sign to the Reverend Stan Levit, who realised the object's importance when Sydney chose to decorate the harbour bridge with Stace's 'Eternity' during the fireworks welcoming in the 21st century. Levit contacted the Museum, which acquired the object in 2000. When the Museum opened at Acton, 'Eternity' was adopted as the title for a gallery exploring the emotional lives of diverse Australians.

Other areas of the Museum's new galleries emerged as the curators engaged with the National Historical Collection built up over the preceding decades. Since its foundation, the Museum has sought to acquire collections illuminating people's interconnections and interactions with Australia's landforms, waterways, fire systems, plants and animals. In 2001, many objects acquired through targeted collecting projects relating to this theme were placed on long-term display for the first time. Among the most touching was the 'Kanangra Express', a wicker and canvas pram used by pioneering environmentalist Myles Dunphy to take his infant son Milo on bushwalks through the Blue Mountains. A few years after Myles died, Milo donated his father's walking and camping equipment to the Museum, together with memorabilia relating to Myles's work campaigning for the creation of the Blue Mountains and Kanangra Boyd national parks.

An ongoing project

Over the past decade, the Museum has continued to develop the National Historical Collection. Recent collecting projects have focused on developing holdings of early Australian colonial material and acquiring objects relating to important events and people in Australian history, in keeping with the Museum's standing as a leading Australian cultural institution. The Museum recently acquired highly significant items such as a small work table crafted from timber sent by First Fleet Surgeon-General John White to his patron in London in 1791; one of the few surviving items of clothing issued to convicts; and Robert O'Hara Burke's water bottle, which was recovered from Cooper Creek after the explorer perished there.

Museum curators keep a keen eye on auction catalogues, where well-known objects sometimes come up for purchase. At recent sales the Museum has acquired a rare copy of Ned Kelly's Jerilderie letter; the 1867 Melbourne Cup — an elaborate silver trophy won by a horse with the intriguing name of Tim Whiffler; and the poignant illuminated address presented by Wurundjeri headman William Barak to former premier Graham Berry in 1886 on the occasion of him leaving, to thank him for his support of the Coranderrk Aboriginal Station. Berry apparently kept the address and it passed down through his family until it was purchased from a house clearing sale and then eventually put up for auction.

The Museum has also benefited from the generosity of families such as the Faithfull and Maple-Brown families of Springfield station in New South Wales. William Pitt Faithfull first settled at Springfield in the 1830s and he and his family became inveterate collectors, keeping items from generations of everyday life and creating a family museum in their house. In 2003, Faithfull's descendants offered to donate much of this material to the Museum. The collection came to more than 1500 objects, including a number of women's dresses dating from the early 1800s to the early 1900s. One of the most striking is a woollen dress with lace trim, purchased by one of the Faithfull girls from the David Jones department store in Sydney. At the time, Springfield was exporting large amounts of fine wool to Britain for textile manufacture and it is intriguing to wonder if some of it found its way back to Australia and to Springfield as a beautiful pink dress.

Every second Wednesday morning, the Museum's Acquisitions and Collections Group, including senior curatorial, conservation and registration staff, gathers to consider the latest round of proposals for objects to be added to the Museum's collection. The list usually includes some of the approximately 30 unsolicited collection offers the Museum now receives each week from the public. Curators add proposals for objects they have located through community contacts or research projects and argue for items coming up for auction around Australia and overseas. Australian Government and other agencies continue occasionally to offer material for transfer to the Museum.

The acquisitions group carefully evaluates each potential new collection. Discussion explores each object's significance, that is, its character, value and rarity as a record of Australia's history, people and culture. Each is considered in terms of how it relates to the existing collection, if it complements or extends existing holdings, addresses gaps or weaknesses or is required for upcoming exhibitions or other programs. Curators are particularly interested in an object's provenance, or what is known about how and where it was made, who owned and used it, and how it has interwoven with people's lives over time. This information enables the Museum to tell, through objects, detailed, personalised stories about Australia's past.

The Museum acquires only a small percentage of the items proposed for its collection. It commits to caring for objects in the National Historical Collection in perpetuity and this means that each potential new acquisition is assessed, not only for its significance as a historical artefact, but also in terms of the resources required to acquire, transport, store and conserve it over the long term. For an object to join the National Historical Collection, it must pass through a rigorous system of assessment and approval and its acceptance into the collection is ultimately ratified by the Museum's governing Council.

In many ways, the National Historical Collection is a living entity. The Museum's core thematic framework provides a basic structure that endures over time, a conceptual architecture that binds together and interrelates diverse kinds of material. Different generations, however, respond to this framework in varying ways, adapting collecting practices to changing understandings of history, shifting cultural priorities and the serendipitous flow of objects in and out of public view. At its heart, the Museum's collection evolves as the institution's staff engage with people around Australia, considering how their stories can be recorded and expressed through the objects that have interwoven with their lives. In this way, the National Historical Collection continues to develop as a democratic collection, shaped to represent the breadth of Australia's environments, peoples and cultures. Objects join the Museum's collection through many different avenues but they come together as an abiding resource through which Australians can better imagine and understand themselves.

Kirsten Wehner
Senior Curator

This essay draws on my colleagues' research and publications, and particularly senior curator Guy Hansen's 'Collecting for a nation', in *Captivating and Curious: Celebrating the collections of the National Museum of Australia*, National Museum of Australia Press, 2005.

THE COLLECTION

JOHN GORE'S TELESCOPE

From the 1660s, with no land borders to defend, most of Britain's military spending went on the Royal Navy and helped stimulate great achievements in the related fields of navigation, astronomy and optics. These advances, embodied in John Gore's telescope, would make Britain the world's leading maritime power from the eighteenth century.

Captain Gore, an American-born Royal Navy officer, sailed to the Pacific four times between 1764 and 1780 under captains Byron, Wallis, Cook and Clerke. Gore observed the Transit of Venus at Tahiti in 1769 and, following the deaths of Cook and Clerke during Cook's third Pacific voyage, assumed command and brought the expedition home.

Gore's Dollond day and night telescope, handed down through his family and donated to the Museum in 2006 by direct descendant Jack Gallaway, is fitted with an achromatic lens. Among their many uses at sea, telescopes were employed in astronomical observations to determine longitude, but the chromatic distortions inherent in their lenses compromised their accuracy. The achromatic lens, patented by London optician John Dollond in 1758, produced a clear, sharp image and made observations, and therefore navigation, more accurate.

Gore's telescope was made sometime between 1761 and 1783, and would have been a very expensive instrument. During his voyages, Gore used his remarkable skill as a marksman to collect natural history specimens. With 'scientific gentlemen' eager to acquire curiosities from the newly discovered regions of the world, Gore would have been able to supplement his navy pay.

Portrait of Captain John Gore 1780 by John Webber
National Library of Australia

Two interchangeable eyepieces from John Gore's telescope 1760s

JAMES COOK'S BUST

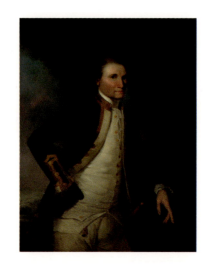

In the 1770s and 1780s, Captain James Cook's fame spread beyond Britain as readers throughout Europe devoured the translated accounts of his three Pacific voyages. Veneration of Cook's achievements even transcended France's and Britain's fierce imperial rivalry, as this French neo-classical marble bust of the celebrated navigator shows. The bust reproduces in the round the bas-relief portrait of Cook by acclaimed French sculptor Augustin Pajou. Pajou's portrait, completed in 1788, was commissioned for a cenotaph to Cook built for the Marquis Jean-Joseph de Laborde in the extensive gardens of his château at Méréville.

De Laborde, a wealthy French financier, patron of the arts and banker to the Court of Louis XVI, shared his sovereign's fascination with navigation and discovery. Two of his sons had sailed with La Pérouse on his voyage of exploration undertaken in 1785 in emulation of Cook's voyages. Both Edouard and Ange-Auguste de Laborde drowned in Canadian waters in 1786, and their father had a 'column rostrale' (a nautically themed memorial) built in their memory on a small island in the middle of a lake in his garden, effectively linking them to the career and achievements of Captain Cook.

It's likely this marble bust is a copy of the one in the cenotaph, made at about the same time by one of Pajou's circle. The Museum purchased the sculpture in 2007.

Portrait of Captain James Cook 1782
by John Webber
National Portrait Gallery

French marble portrait bust of Captain Jacques Cook about 1788

SIR ANDREW SNAPE HAMOND'S TABLE

This small Pembroke worktable illustrates patronage and trade links in the colony. In 1791, the First Fleet's Surgeon-General, John White, sent his patron in London, Sir Andrew Snape Hamond, some planks cut from a tree growing near the new settlement at Port Jackson. Hamond, Commissioner of the Navy, had secured White's appointment to the First Fleet. White's gift of rare, exotic and highly desirable timber acknowledged the help he had already received. It would also have helped him retain Hamond's ongoing favour and interest in White's career.

The wood was known in the colony as 'beefwood', because the newly cut timber resembled freshly sliced salt beef. In London, a cabinet-maker cut the precious timber into thin veneers to top this small Pembroke worktable. Such tables, made in the fashionable neo-classical style of the late eighteenth and early nineteenth centuries, have hinged, fold-down sides and two drawers, and were used for writing, taking tea and playing games.

A label in Hamond's hand, found pasted inside one of the drawers, records the table's origin. It reads: 'Sent from Botany Bay by Dr ~~Brown~~ White Surgeon of the Navy — in Planks & this table made up in London — Beef Wood'. The table sat in the drawing room of the Hamond family home in Norfolk, England, for more than 200 years before being purchased by the Museum in 2006.

Sir Andrew Snape Hamond 1830
by George Henry Phillips
National Portrait Gallery, London

The First Fleet table
1790s

GOVERNOR KING'S SNUFFBOX

A silver snuffbox presented to New South Wales Governor Philip Gidley King by Lieutenant James Grant in 1801 is one of the earliest pieces of silverwork made in the colony of New South Wales. Engraved with the initials 'PGK', the underside of the lid is inscribed: 'Lt. Grant to Governor King June 4 1801'.

King arrived in Port Jackson with the First Fleet in 1788 and was governor of New South Wales from 1800 until 1806, when he was succeeded by Captain William Bligh.

King received the snuffbox from Grant to mark King George III's birthday, 4 June 1801, after an exploratory voyage to the Bass Strait. The tiny oval-shaped snuffbox, just 6 centimetres long, may have been presented to King in appreciation of his patronage — or perhaps Grant was trying to maintain favour with the governor.

Grant's own role in the fledgling colony was also significant. Six days after presenting the snuff box to King, he set out to explore the Hunter region, an expedition that led to the settlement of Newcastle. After returning from the Hunter, Grant sat on the bench for the trial of a naval officer accused of assaulting John Macarthur. In 1803, after his return to England, Grant published *Narrative of a Voyage of Discovery*.

The snuffbox demonstrates the importance of patronage in the development of colonial society in Australia and is strongly connected to key features of King's governorship, notably his focus on exploration, settlement and industry.

Lieut. Philip Gidley King in 1789
National Archives of Australia

Snuffbox given to Governor King by Lieutenant Grant 1801

THE INVESTIGATOR'S STREAM ANCHOR

In 1801 accomplished navigator Matthew Flinders set sail on board the *Investigator* to explore and chart the Australian coastline. He sailed through the Recherche Archipelago, a group of hundreds of islands and rocky outcrops in dangerous waters off the south coast of Western Australia, twice during his celebrated circumnavigation of Australia.

Flinders reached Middle Island, the largest island near the centre of the group, in January 1802. Here the ship's botanist and artists collected and documented the landscape, flora and fauna. The crew collected water and salt, and Cape Barren geese made a welcome addition to their diet. After three days the *Investigator* sailed east.

Returning a year later, after long months of restricted diet, Flinders and his crew were suffering from dysentery and scurvy. Hoping to replenish fresh food, water and supplies, they stopped at Middle Island, but found only a few geese and were forced to leave largely empty-handed. While setting sail, the ship's anchors did not hold in the gusty conditions and the cables had to be cut to stop the *Investigator* being pulled towards the rocks. Flinders lost two anchors and barely avoided shipwreck.

The *Investigator*'s stream anchor, along with the best bower anchor, lay in the relatively undisturbed waters off Middle Island for 170 years. They were recovered in 1973 by an expedition from the Underwater Explorers' Club of Adelaide, South Australia, led by Doug Seton. The 2.5-metre stream anchor, which weighs 400 kilograms, became the property of the Australian Government and, in 1981, it was transferred to the Museum from the Department of Transport.

H.M. Sloop Investigator *1802*
by Geoffrey C Ingleton
National Library of Australia

The *Investigator*'s stream anchor 1801

GEORGE RANKEN'S LANDAU

This early nineteenth-century landau, known as the 'Ranken Coach', was first owned by George Ranken, a prosperous Scot who settled in Bathurst during the 1820s. Believed to be one of the oldest surviving horse-drawn vehicles in Australia, the wooden carriage is painted black and has padded, leather-covered bench seats facing front and back, a convertible top that opens in the middle, glass and solid window panels on the doors, and a seat at the front for the driver.

George Ranken migrated from Scotland to New South Wales with his wife Janet in 1821–22. The family settled on a 2000-acre land grant known as Kelloshiel, outside Bathurst. Over the next 30 years Ranken enlarged his estates and experimented with producing flour, cheese, wine and beer, as well as running cattle and sheep, and breeding horses. Ranken died while on a business venture to London in October 1860, and the landau was then sold to Sebastian Hodge of Bathurst.

Like Ranken, Hodge prospered in the young colony, eventually owning a timberyard and joinery business, a skating rink and an undertaker's business. The landau was used as a mourning vehicle until it was replaced by a motor vehicle in the 1920s.

In 1925, the landau was presented to the Royal Australian Historical Society and placed on display in Vaucluse House. It was used in the 'March to Nationhood' pageant on the opening day of the 1938 sesquicentenary celebrations in Sydney. It was later displayed at the Old Sydney Town open air museum and theme park before being purchased by the Museum in 1980.

The Ranken coach 1821

CONVICT-ERA SHIRT AND PUNISHMENT SHOE

Between 1830 and 1836, a group of convicts employed on a secondary punishment project at Granton, 19 kilometres north of Hobart, quarried more than two million tonnes of soil, stone and clay. They used it to construct a 13-kilometres-long causeway over the River Derwent, a convict barracks, the Black Snake Inn and their Commandant's cottage. Most of the convicts worked in heavy leg-irons, which only a blacksmith could remove.

When the Commandant's cottage, completed in 1830, was renovated 130 years later, a remarkable discovery was made: the builders had hidden a shirt inside a cavity in the wall near the chimney, and a shoe under the floor near the fireplace. The centuries-old British folk magic practice of deliberately concealing objects such as shoes, clothing, witch bottles, mummified cats and animal skulls in houses during construction had travelled to Australia with its practitioners. Such 'house sacrifices' were often placed near chimneys, to prevent entry by witches and evil spirits.

Despite being issued in great numbers to convicts and other workers during the transportation era, the shirt is one of only three to be discovered in Australia, and is the best preserved. Still stiff with starch, the shirt was probably new and unworn when rolled tightly and walled up. The shoe, made from hand-stitched leather, with iron hobnails hammered into the sole and heel, is known as a 'punishment shoe'. Its sides have been cut away to allow the wearer's leg-irons to cut into his ankle.

The shirt and shoe, along with other objects found in the grounds of the cottage, were purchased by the Museum in 2005.

Punishment shoe about 1830

Convict-era shirt about 1830

THOMAS ALSOP'S
CONVICT LOVE TOKEN

In 1833 Thomas Alsop, a 21-year-old brick labourer, was convicted at Staffordshire for stealing a sheep. Alsop was sentenced to transportation for life, and sailed for Van Diemen's Land (Tasmania) on the *Moffatt* on 29 January 1834. While Alsop awaited his transportation he had at least two 'love tokens' made to leave behind: one for his mother and one for an unknown person.

Immediately on arrival in the colony, Alsop was assigned to a chain gang. His record shows that between 1836 and 1847 he committed numerous offences, including attempting to abscond, refusing to work, stealing cattle, representing himself as a constable and being found in bed with a female prisoner.

Despite his poor conduct record, Alsop was granted a conditional pardon on 7 November 1848 and a full pardon on 5 February 1850.

Alsop married Irish-born Sarah Eliza Kirk, with whom he had a son, Thomas, and a daughter, Sarah. In the 1850s Alsop worked as a fish hawker and lived in Hobart. He died in 1891.

Smoothing and engraving a coin with a message of affection was one of the few ways a convict transported to Australia could leave a memento behind in England. Frequently engraved around the time of conviction for a prisoner's loved one or family, the tokens record personal and emotional responses from convicts whose lives are more often represented by official government records. Over 300 such tokens are held in the Museum's collection.

The reverse of this token reads: 'The rose soon drupes & dies, the brier fades away, but my fond heart for you I love shall never go astray.'

Thomas Alsop's love token made for his mother 1833

The convict railway, Port Arthur about 1926 by John Watt Beattie
Tasmanian Archive and Heritage Office

BATMAN LAND DEED

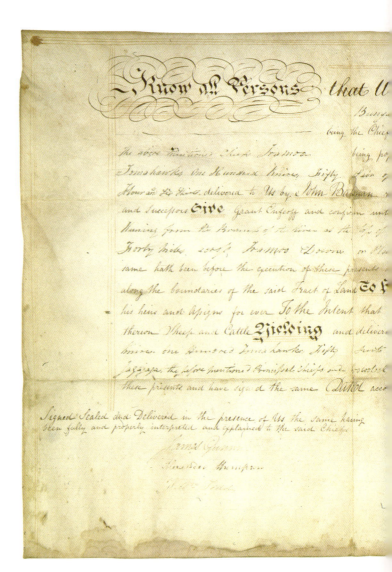

The Batman deeds were drawn up in 1835 by an influential group of settlers from Van Diemen's Land (Tasmania), who wanted large areas of land in the Port Phillip district (Victoria). The group, led by entrepreneur John Batman, struck a deal with the local Kulin people. Batman offered 20 blankets, 30 axes, 100 knives, 50 pairs of scissors, 200 handkerchiefs, 100 pounds (45 kilograms) of flour, six shirts and an annual payment in exchange for 600,000 acres (more than 240,000 hectares) of land.

William Todd, a member of Batman's party, described in his diary how Batman had asked him to get the Aboriginal leaders to make 'a signature of the country and tribe — on the bark of a tree'. Batman transcribed those marks onto the handwritten land deed.

It is unclear how these men understood the document they were signing. They may have believed they were participating in a *tanderrum*, a ceremony that allowed visitors to use Kulin land as long as they were friendly to the local people and respected their laws. This understanding appears to have been confirmed by Batman's use, during negotiations, of a centuries-old mode of conveyancing called feoffment. In feoffment, soil or twigs are passed from the person selling the land to the person buying it — an act that was also part of the Kulin's *tanderrum*.

Despite the agreements, both the colonial authorities in Sydney and the British Government declared the treaty null and void. The legality of the exchange and the subsequent debates over whether it acknowledged or voided Aboriginal ownership of land have continued until the present day.

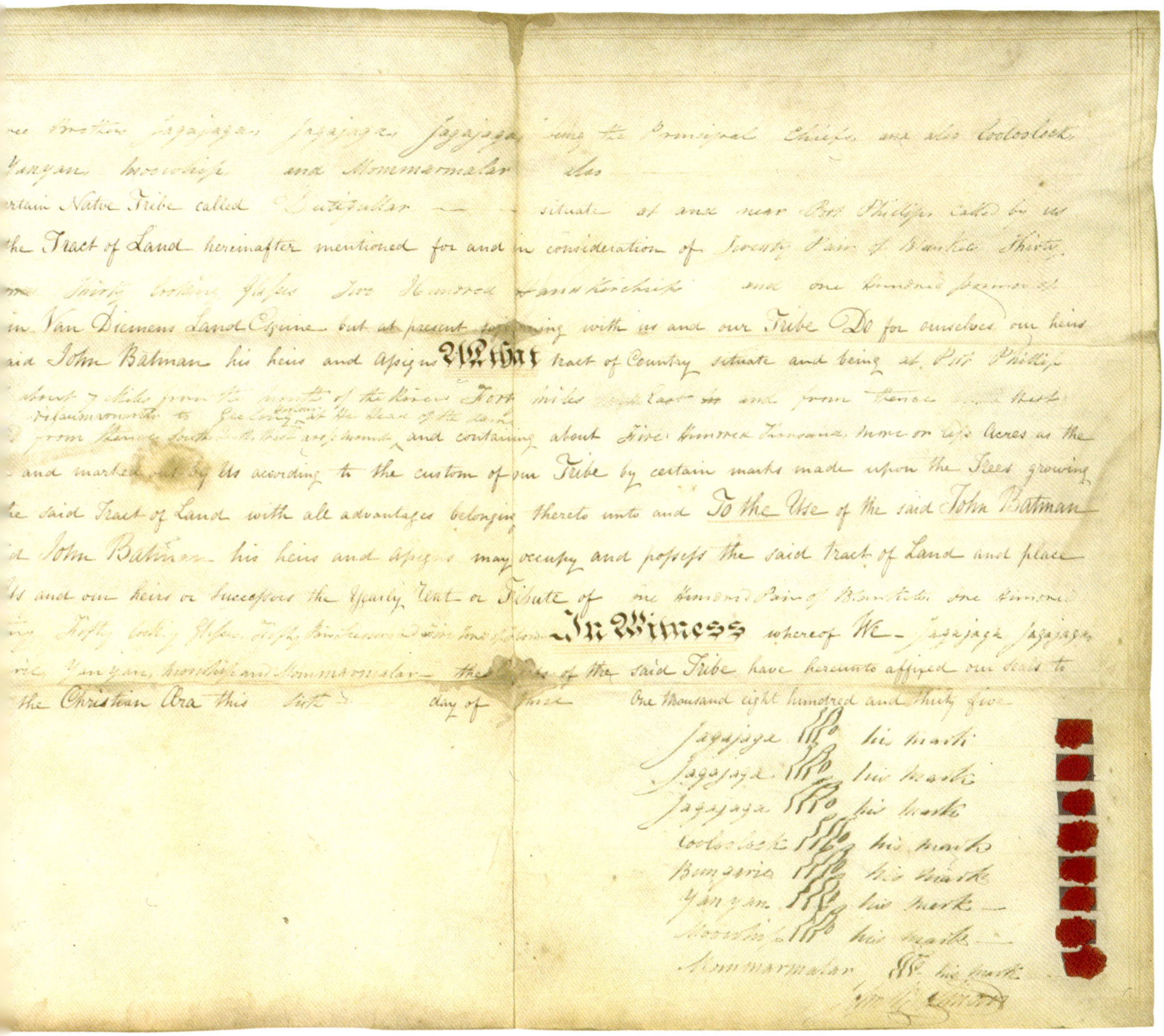

ee brother Jagajaga Jagajaga Jagajaga being the Principal Chiefs and also Cooloolock
Yanyan Moowhip and Mommarmalar also
rtain Native Tribe called Dutigallar — situate at and near Port Phillip called by us
the Tract of Land hereinafter mentioned for and in consideration of Twenty Pair of Blankets Thirty
Thirty looking glasses Two Hundred Handkerchiefs and one hundred pounds of
in Van Diemens Land Esquire but at present sojourning with us and our Tribe Do for ourselves our heirs
id John Batman his heirs and Assigns All that tract of Country situate and being at Port Phillip
about 7 Miles from the mouth of the River Forty miles East and from thence West
from thence South West across and containing about Five Hundred Thousand more or less Acres as the
and marked by Us according to the custom of our Tribe by certain marks made upon the Trees growing
he said Tract of Land with all advantages belonging thereto unto and To the Use of the said John Batman
d John Batman his heirs and Assigns may occupy and possess the said tract of Land and place
Us and our heirs or Successors the Yearly Rent or Tribute of one Hundred Pair of Blankets one Hundred
Fifty looking glasses Fifty Pair Scissors and five Tons of Flour In Witness whereof We Jagajaga Jagajaga
rie Yanyan Moowhip and Mommarmalar the Chiefs of the said Tribe have hereunto affixed our seals to
the Christian Æra this sixth day of June One thousand eight hundred and thirty five

Jagajaga his mark
Jagajaga his mark
Jagajaga his mark
Cooloolock his mark
Bungarie his mark
Yanyan his mark
Moowhip his mark
Mommarmalar his mark

Batman land deed 1835

Batman's Treaty with the Aborigines at Merri Creek, 6th June 1835
about 1875
by John Wesley Burtt
State Library of Victoria

LEICHHARDT NAMEPLATE

The 1848 disappearance of Ludwig Leichhardt and his entire exploration party is one of the great mysteries of Australian history. Many theories have been proposed over the years to explain where Leichhardt died, some concluding he perished somewhere near the Simpson Desert. This small brass nameplate is the only known artefact from his entire expedition.

Ludwig Leichhardt, a German-born scientist and naturalist, arrived in Sydney in 1842 and mounted three expeditions to explore Australia's inland. His explorations and observations of the Australian environment were internationally recognised, and influential in the expansion of the pastoral industry.

Marked 'LUDWIG LEICHHARDT 1848', the nameplate cannot tell us where Leichhardt died but it proves that he made it at least two-thirds of the way across the continent during his east–west crossing attempt. This was a remarkable achievement for a European in 1848. The nameplate was discovered in about 1900 by an Aboriginal man known as 'Jackie', who was working for an outback drover and prospector named Charles Harding. It was attached to a partly burnt firearm in a bottle (boab) tree near Sturt Creek, between the Tanami and Great Sandy deserts, just inside Western Australia near the Northern Territory border. Like a number of trees that have been identified elsewhere, and accepted as having been marked by Leichhardt on his fatal attempt to cross the continent in 1848, the boab tree was inscribed with an 'L'.

In about 1918, Harding gave the nameplate to a friend, Reginald Bristow-Smith. The Museum purchased the nameplate from the Bristow-Smith family in 2006.

Leichhardt nameplate
1848

Portrait of Ludwig Leichhardt about 1850
National Library of Australia

MAJOR SIR THOMAS MITCHELL'S DUELLING PISTOLS

Major Sir Thomas Mitchell played an important role in the early exploration of colonial Australia. Born in Scotland, he trained as a surveyor in the army before moving to Australia to take up his appointment as Surveyor General of the colony in 1827. He remained in this position until his death.

Mitchell was responsible for exploring vast areas of south-eastern Australia and opening up new grazing lands in the southern parts of Victoria. His contribution to the surveying of Australia saw him knighted in 1838. An accomplished artist, botanist and poet, Mitchell is also remembered for his 'hot-headed' temper. It is speculated that he is the last person in Australia to ever challenge anyone to a duel.

At dawn on 27 September 1851, Mitchell confronted Sir Stuart Alexander Donaldson in Sydney. He had issued the challenge because Donaldson had publicly criticised the over-expenditure of the Surveyor General's Department. Both duellists missed their mark — only Donaldson's hat was damaged in the altercation. Their seconds stepped in to declare that honour had been satisfied, and the duel was abandoned.

The Royal Australian Historical Society records that these were the pistols used in the duel. The Museum purchased the pistols from the society in 1983.

Major Sir Thomas Mitchell's duelling pistols used in 1851

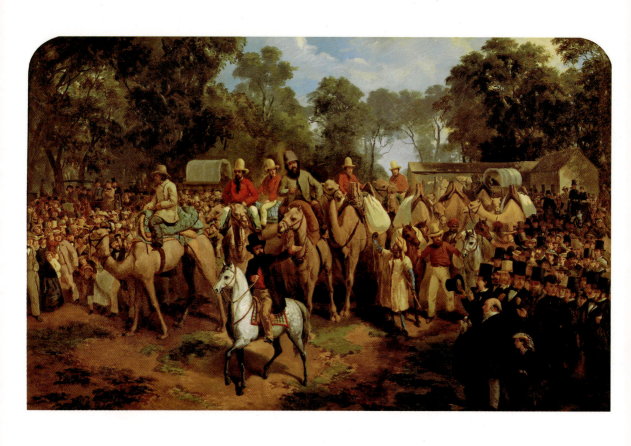

ROBERT O'HARA BURKE'S WATER BOTTLE

As an item that helped Robert O'Hara Burke cross great stretches of dry terrain, this leather water bottle represents the challenges faced by explorers during the colonial period as they engaged with the brutal reality of inland Australia.

The Victorian Exploring Expedition, usually known as the Burke and Wills expedition, remains one of the most celebrated journeys of Australian land exploration. An initiative of the Royal Society of Victoria, the costly and well-provisioned expedition sought to be the first to cross the continent from south to north.

The expedition left Melbourne for the Gulf of Carpentaria in August 1860, led by Burke. Second-in-command William John Wills was the surveyor and astronomer. At Menindie, Burke appointed William Wright in charge and left for Cooper Creek. He grew impatient waiting for Wright to arrive with the supplies and, on 16 December 1860, Burke and Wills left Cooper Creek to make a dash for the northern shoreline. They eventually encountered salty marshes and a shifting tide, and could proceed no further. Even though they could not see the open water, they had reached their goal.

The return journey proved fatal. Burke and Wills limped back to the Cooper Creek camp only to find that the rest of the depot party had departed just hours earlier. They died attempting to reach Mount Hopeless.

The Museum bought the water bottle at auction at Sotheby's in 2005 after it was offered for sale by the Burke Cole family. Research shows that a search party led by Alfred Howitt in September 1861 retrieved the water bottle soon after Burke and Wills died at Cooper Creek, and that the bottle originally belonged to Burke.

Memorandum of the Start of the Exploring Expedition 1860 by Nicholas Chevalier
Art Gallery of South Australia

Leather water bottle belonging to Robert O'Hara Burke about 1860

TIM WHIFFLER'S MELBOURNE CUP

In 1867 a 'beautiful bright bay' thoroughbred called Tim Whiffler won both the Melbourne Cup and the Queen's Plate. He was trained by the renowned Etienne de Mestre, who eventually claimed five Melbourne Cup victories, a record that lasted a century.

Tim Whiffler was probably named after the fictional winner of the Melbourne Cup in Adam Lindsay Gordon's 1865 poem, 'Hippodromania'. The name was so popular that two Tim Whifflers ran in the 1867 cup. To avoid confusion, the bookmakers referred to them as 'Sydney Tim' and 'Melbourne Tim'. Sydney Tim was installed as favourite and went on to win. Melbourne Tim finished fifth.

The Victorian Racing Club commissioned the 1867 Melbourne Cup from London firm WR Smily & Co. for £100. Victorian jewellers were outraged at the use of non-Australian artisans to make the cup trophy and sent a petition of complaint to the Victorian Racing Club. They argued that a local silversmith, William Edwards, had produced a trophy that was superior in both design and workmanship to the imported trophy. The controversy might be why the club did not present another Melbourne Cup trophy for almost a decade.

Instead, Edwards' trophy was awarded to the winner of the 1867 Queen's Plate, run two days after the Melbourne Cup. Since both races were won by Tim Whiffler, the trophies remained in the same family collection for almost 150 years, until purchased by the Museum at auction in October 2011.

Tim Whiffler sketched by ST Gill after winning the 1867 Melbourne Cup
Illustrated Sydney News, 16 November 1867
State Library of Victoria

Melbourne Cup trophy won by Tim Whiffler
1867

PADDLE STEAMER ENTERPRISE

Built in Echuca, Victoria, in 1878, the Paddle Steamer *Enterprise* is one of the oldest working paddle steamers in the world. It was made from river red gums, which were plentiful along the Murray River and provided hardwood for building and powering the hundreds of paddle steamers that dominated the rivers of south-eastern Australia from the 1860s to the early 1900s.

The *Enterprise* is known as a 'shallow drafter', because there is very little of it sitting below the water line — a mere 75 centimetres. This made it suitable for dealing with the varying water levels of the Murray–Darling river systems as it towed barges loaded with wool and supplies between towns and busy ports.

Over the years, the *Enterprise* had a number of different owners and many changes and adjustments were made to the vessel. Augustus Creager bought the *Enterprise* in 1919 and raised his young family on board while working as a fisherman. From the 1930s he was assisted by his wife Hilda, one of the few women at the time to hold a commercial fishing licence. Living on the water did have its hazards for the Creager children. As toddlers, each of them fell overboard at least once.

In 1984, the *Enterprise* was purchased by the Museum. It was restored in Echuca, before being moved to its new home on Lake Burley Griffin in Canberra. The *Enterprise* is staffed by a dedicated crew of volunteers. Working with Museum conservators, they ensure the ship is maintained in working order and that valuable skills of a bygone era are preserved.

The PS *Enterprise* at full steam on Lake Burley Griffin in Canberra 2003

PS *Enterprise* in the Mannum Dock, South Australia about 1900

NED KELLY'S JERILDERIE LETTER

Bushranger, murderer and stock thief, Ned Kelly is arguably Australia's best-known historical character. His transformation from petty criminal into legendary bushranger began in October 1878 when three policemen were shot dead by the Kelly gang at Stringybark Creek. The Victorian Government responded by outlawing Ned and Dan Kelly, Steve Hart and Joe Byrne, which meant they could be shot on sight by anybody at any time.

For two years the gang roamed freely through north-eastern Victoria and the Riverina, robbing the banks at Euroa and Jerilderie. Finally, at Glenrowan in June 1880, they donned suits of armour to make a dramatic but doomed stand against the Victorian police. Dan Kelly, Hart and Byrne were killed and Ned Kelly was taken prisoner.

Tried and found guilty for the murder of Constable Lonigan at Stringybark Creek, Kelly was hanged at Melbourne Gaol on the morning of 11 November 1880.

Kelly is the only bushranger known to have left a detailed written justification of his actions, and his 'manifesto' is regarded by many as an early call for a republican Australia. The 56-page document reflects the voice of a man who feels he has been deeply wronged. He admits to crimes but claims he was forced into them by a corrupt police force. He demands that squatters share their property with the poor.

The document ends with a violent threat against all who oppose him: 'I am a Widow's Son, outlawed and my orders must be obeyed'. Copies of the document were made by the police and by publican John Hanlon. Hanlon's transcription of the Jerilderie letter was purchased by the Museum in 2001.

A prison portrait of Ned Kelly 1873

John Hanlon's transcription of Ned Kelly's Jerilderie letter 1879

All those that have reason to fear me had better sell out and give £10 out of every hundred to the widow and orphan fund and do not attempt to reside in Victoria but as short a time as possible after reading this notice neglect this and abide by the consequence which shall be worse than rust in wheat in Victoria or the drought of a dry season to the grasshoppers in N. S. Wales I do not wish to give the order full force without giving timely warning but I am a widow's son, outlawed and my orders must be obeyed

NELSON'S DOG COLLAR

This copper collar with brass studs is linked to the dramatic story of a dog saving a cab-driver from drowning in a Melbourne street in the 1880s.

Melbourne's location, close to the Yarra River, made it prone to flooding. On the evening of 15 November 1881, a thunderstorm brought heavy rain to the city, turning streets into miniature rivers. Thomas Brown, the driver of a horsedrawn cab, was pulled into a torrent racing down Swanston Street.

Brown's cries for help were heard by local tobacconist and hairdresser William Higginbotham and his dog, Nelson. Luckily for Brown, Nelson was a Newfoundland, a breed with a strong instinct for water rescue and retrieval, a large, powerful body, water-resistant coat and webbed feet.

Nelson made repeated attempts to catch hold of Brown, persisting even when the cab-driver was sucked into a culvert and given up for dead. In a final effort, Higginbotham, another man, Mr Mates, and Nelson plunged into the racing stream and managed to haul Brown out of the water. Bleeding and with his clothes torn to shreds, Brown was taken to hospital, but was not badly injured.

Higginbotham and Nelson took weeks to get over the dramatic rescue and never recovered their health. Nelson, who was well-known to many inner city Melburnians as he used to sit outside Higginbotham's shop, later led a fire brigade parade where the collar was presented to him in recognition of the feat. The collar was purchased by the Museum in 2011, 130 years after the rescue. Conservation analysis reveals that the collar was once nickel plated and shone like silver.

Collar presented to Nelson the Newfoundland 1881

William John Higginbotham with dog, Nelson about 1880
courtesy Russ Higginbotham

MISS FAITHFULL'S WOOL DRESS

William and Mary Pitt Faithfull established Springfield station, near Goulburn in New South Wales, as a merino stud in 1838. By the mid-1880s, when this pink dress was made, wool was Australia's most important export and Springfield was flourishing.

Locally, a small textile industry needing coarse wool for furnishings and rough clothing was developing, and British mills producing quality textiles were demanding as much fine merino wool as Australia could grow. William Faithfull's son Lucian bred flocks that produced fleece for both these markets, ensuring the family's prosperity and their place among the colony's social elite.

In about 1885, one of the Faithfulls' three girls, Florence, Constance or Lilian, bought this fine wool dress with bodice and skirt from the David Jones department store in Sydney. By the 1870s, David Jones was offering shopping by post, sending out coloured postcards and seasonal fashion catalogues complete with fabric samples and instructions for how to measure oneself. The Faithfulls of Springfield regularly took advantage of this service.

Representing the latest in British fashion, the pink dress wasn't a very practical garment for a hot, dusty Australian sheep station. Miss Faithfull would have worn it visiting friends, taking a carriage ride or perhaps shopping in Sydney.

The dress was donated through the Australian Government's Cultural Gifts Program by James IF Maple-Brown, Diana Boyd and Pamela Maple-Brown in 2005.

Lilian Faithfull of Springfield station
about 1883

Miss Faithfull's 'pink merino' bustle dress
about 1885

KIMBERLEY POINTS

The Museum cares for a highly-prized collection of tools and trade items from north-west Australia, of which the Kimberley points form an important part.

'Points' were traditionally made from stone and used for the tips of spears and as exchange items. After European settlement Aboriginal people were quick to make use of new materials such as glass and ceramics: they were easier to work with, gave a very sharp edge and were relatively accessible.

The arrival of new types of raw materials encouraged adaptation and innovation in Kimberley point manufacture. Made from old glass bottles and ceramics from telegraph insulators, as well as stone, the Kimberley points reflect the skill of their makers, who detached very tiny flakes using a pressure-flaking technique to produce long and symmetrical forms. The consistent flaking properties of glass meant points could be longer and more finely shaped than those made from stone.

The importance of the points as trade items derived from their connection with the Dreaming, which conferred upon them a special status and value in the ceremonial exchange system within the Kimberley and beyond.

A display of Kimberley points at the National Museum of Australia

WILLIAM BARAK'S ILLUMINATED ADDRESS

On 24 March 1886 a group of men from Coranderrk, led by William Barak, travelled to Melbourne to farewell former premier Graham Berry, who was returning to England. In the Executive Council Chamber they presented him with gifts of spears, boomerangs and other artefacts, along with this illuminated address. Drafted by Barak and signed by 16 Coranderrk leaders, the address and gifts acknowledged Berry's assistance in maintaining the station in 1881, against the advice of the Aboriginal Protection Board.

Born in 1824, William Barak was an Aboriginal leader whose skills as a diplomat are legendary. The words of Barak's address are a powerful Aboriginal voice from that time:

'When the Board would not give us much food and clothes and wanted to drive us off the land we came to you and told you our trouble and you gave us the land for our own as long as we live and gave us more food and clothes and Blankets and Better houses and the people all very thankful ... We give you small present with our love, when you go away keep remembering the Natives for the Natives will remember you for your doing good to Coranderrk.'

The illuminated address bridges the two cultures in which Barak lived and reveals his great talent as a mediator. It also demonstrates the Coranderrk residents' sophisticated engagement with the colony's political structure.

In February 2009, in the same Executive Council Chamber, Museum staff presented reproductions of the address to descendants of the Wurundjeri who were present in 1886.

A group of men at Coranderrk Station, Healesville
State Library of Victoria

William Barak's illuminated address
1886

To the Honbl. Graham Berry.

Melbourne, March 22nd/86.

We have come to see you because you have done a great deal of work for the Aborigines.

I feel very sorrowful and first time I hear you was going home I was crying, you do all that thing for the Station when we were in trouble. when the Board would not give us much food and clothes and wanted to drive us off the land we come to you and told you our trouble and you gave us the land for our own as long as we live and gave us more food and clothes and blankets and better houses and the people all very thankful.

And now you leave this country, Victoria to go to England where we may never see you no more, we give you small present with our love, when you go away keep remembering the Natives for the Natives will remember you for your doing good to Coranderrk.

We had a trouble here in this country but we can all meet up along Our Father we hope that God will lead you right through the water and take you safe to England and keep you in the straight way and give you eternal life through Jesus Christ Our Saviour.

Signed Barak ×
Chief of the Yarra Yarra tribe of Aborigines,
Victoria Australia.

Bertdrak ×	Mooney +	Patterson ×
Katacarmen +	Manton ×	Coyle
Wort se ilum +	Hamilton +	Stewart ×
Ngiaqueon +	Rowan ×	Logan
Derrinil ×	Were ×	Gable ×

BUDD BILLY'S BREASTPLATE

Lachlan Macquarie became Governor of New South Wales in 1810. By 1814, relations between the colonists and Aboriginal people in the area around Sydney had deteriorated and people were being killed on both sides. In an attempt to combat this situation, Macquarie developed a number of strategies to bring about peaceful relations between the two groups, rewarding friendly Aboriginal people but treating harshly those who defied the invasion of their lands.

The strategy that had the most lasting impact was the establishment of a 'chieftainship'. While Aboriginal groups have democratic systems based around consensus decision-making by a group of elders, Macquarie wanted a system whereby each 'tribe' had a chief who would settle internal matters and be the intermediary between his 'tribe' and the government. These chiefs were presented with a brass, crescent-shaped 'badge of distinction' engraved with their name and tribe and clearly identifying them and their status. Today, these badges are commonly referred to as 'breastplates'.

This simple brass breastplate, inscribed 'Budd Billy II, King of Jarvis Bay', is one of a significant collection of 65 Aboriginal breastplates held by the Museum. It is notable because it is the only breastplate from the collection for which there is a known photograph of a man wearing his breastplate. In a rustic setting, Budd Billy strikes a semi-formal pose beside his seated wife, Mary Carpenter. Edmund Milne, who collected the breastplate, pasted the photograph into his album.

Breastplates are truly cross-cultural historical items and are illustrative of Aboriginal–European relations from colonial times until well into the twentieth century.

'Budd Billy and his Wangan/Last King and Queen of Jervis Bay 1904'

'Budd Billy II, King of Jarvis Bay' breastplate
about 1896

KLONDIKE FLAG

A hand-painted flag was Charlie Lloyd's only souvenir of his journey to the Klondike goldfields in north-western Canada in 1898.

The Klondike was one of the greatest, but also most brutal, of the gold rushes. Men hauled their supplies over mountain passes, navigated wild rapids and endured arctic conditions — even before reaching the goldfields. Many died, by avalanche, accident or starvation, and very few found enough gold to make the trip worthwhile. Although an experienced and successful goldminer, Lloyd failed to strike it lucky and returned home declaring the whole thing a waste of time.

What Lloyd, and many like him, did discover was a sense of being Australian. Prior to the journey, Lloyd probably would have referred to himself as a Victorian but, on the other side of the world, colonial boundaries meant little. On the frozen goldfields of Canada, Australian miners began to develop a sense of national identity.

When Lloyd and five compatriots commissioned a boat to take them to Dawson City, they named it the *Kangaroo* and chose the 'Advance Australia Arms', a common colonial symbol, to fly from the mast. According to Lloyd, 'it was a devil of a job to give the Yankee an idea of a kangaroo', but using the tiny image in the corner of a Victorian Miners' Right, they managed.

The Lloyd family kept the 'Klondike flag' safe for 113 years. Purchased in 2011, the flag is now part of the Museum's collection.

Klondike flag 1898

OSCAR'S SKETCHBOOK

When staff from the Museum were investigating uncatalogued collections in the early 1990s, they came across a cardboard box containing items once owned by the Institute of Anatomy. At the bottom of this box lay a small exercise book labelled 'Drawn by Oscar, Cooktown boy, aged 18 years'.

The extraordinary set of 40 pencil drawings found inside were depictions of a young Aboriginal man's memories of growing up in far north Queensland. Oscar's sketches depict a variety of scenes from traditional ceremonies and warfare to interactions with Europeans, a rare record of life in the late 1800s from an Aboriginal person's perspective.

Augustus Henry Glissan, manager of Rocklands station and Oscar's overseer, gave Oscar the blue-lined exercise book in 1898. Glissan wrote an index interpreting the drawings and sent the completed book, with an accompanying letter, to family friend Dr Charles Bage in Melbourne in 1899. Bage passed the book on to his colleague Sir Colin MacKenzie, whose collection was to become the nucleus of the Australian Institute of Anatomy, and later the National Museum of Australia.

Oscar's life was perhaps typical for his time and place. The 1873 Palmer River gold rush caused disruptions and violence to traditional Indigenous life in far north-east Queensland and led to dispossession from tribal lands. Obtained by Glissan as a stockman from the police in Cooktown, to work at Rocklands station, near Camooweal, Oscar was forced to adapt to a completely different way of life. What is unique in Oscar's story is that he was encouraged to record his life in drawings, and equally remarkable is the fact that his small book has been preserved.

'Men dressed for the Corroberee. Sketch depicting four male figures in costume', drawing from Oscar's sketchbook about 1899

Oscar's sketchbook about 1899

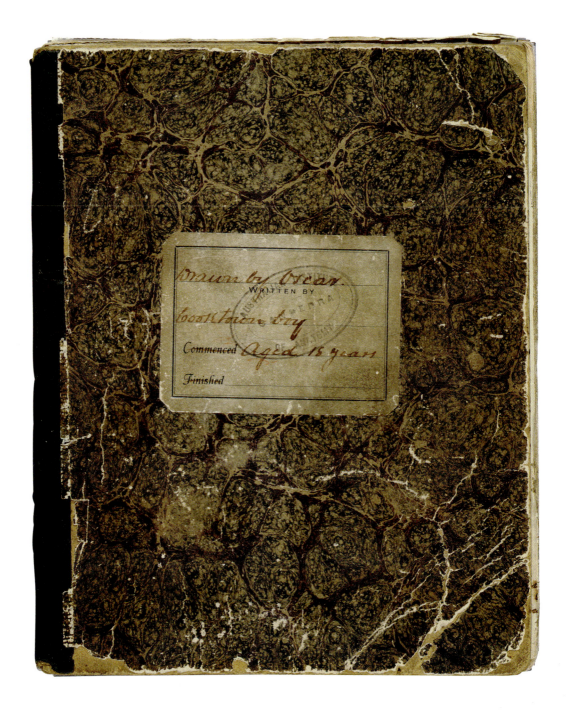

DALLY MESSENGER'S REPRESENTATIVE CAP

This New South Wales Rugby Football League representative cap was presented to Herbert 'Dally' Messenger in 1907.

Messenger's football career started as a five-eighth with the Eastern Suburbs Rugby Union Club in 1905. A player of rare talent, he quickly attracted a strong following among fans. In 1906 he was selected to play for New South Wales and, in 1907, he became a member of the Australian representative rugby union team, the Wallabies.

Towards the end of 1907 Messenger decided to switch his loyalties to the newly established New South Wales Rugby Football League. A rising talent in rugby union, with considerable appeal to fans, his defection to rugby league added credibility to the new code. Messenger quickly emerged as rugby league's first superstar, taking on legendary status within the game. His contribution to the sport is still recognised today in the Dally M Medal, awarded annually to Australian rugby league's best player of the year.

In the early days of rugby league, players selected for state and national teams received embroidered and tasselled caps, hence the term, being 'capped'. This tradition was born of other colonial sports such as cricket and rugby union. This cap was issued to Messenger following his selection for the New South Wales representative side that clashed with the touring team from New Zealand in late 1907.

New South Wales Rugby Football League representative cap presented to Dally Messenger 1907

Portrait of Dally Messenger taken for the 1908–09 Kangaroos tour of England
courtesy Ian Heads

SUNSHINE HARVESTER

This horse-drawn Sunshine stripper harvester was one of 2161 made at the Sunshine Harvester Works in 1911.

Located west of Melbourne, the Sunshine Harvester Works was an agricultural implements factory established by Hugh Victor McKay. The factory was named after McKay's well known stripper harvester, the Sunshine harvester. In 1908, the township of Braybrook Junction, where the factory was located, was renamed Sunshine after the factory.

McKay did not invent the stripper harvester, but his Sunshine model was among the first commercially successful stripper harvesters and changed Australian grain harvesting techniques. Requiring very little skill to operate, the machine could strip, thresh, winnow and bag grain in one operation. It increased grain yields and cut down on the amount of physical labour, as well as the time needed to harvest.

By the 1920s the factory was the largest agricultural implements manufacturer in the Southern Hemisphere, employing over 2500 workers. As well as the Sunshine harvester, the works also manufactured other agricultural implements, supplying farmers across Australia and the world.

In 1992, the Museum purchased this Sunshine harvester from Wood Dale, a farm in New South Wales. Here, the harvester was used until the mid-1950s when the family upgraded some of their farming equipment. For the next 40 years, it was stored in a shed on the property.

Sunshine harvester 1911

Horse-drawn Sunshine harvester about 1930
University of Adelaide Archives

HERBERT BASEDOW'S PHOTOGRAPH

Herbert Basedow — anthropologist, geologist, scientist, explorer and medical practitioner — used photography to document the people and places he encountered across central and northern Australia in the early decades of the twentieth century.

His photographs, mostly taken during his many expeditions in remote Australia, reveal his diverse interests and provide poignant reflections of expeditionary and frontier life. But what sets Basedow apart is the range and diversity of the places he visited.

Basedow travelled to remote regions in central and northern Australia, to places rarely seen even today. He explored a wide range of often rugged and challenging terrains, from wetlands and desert landscapes to severely drought-stricken areas. His photographs provide an exceptional record of these regions in the early twentieth century.

Aboriginal people feature prominently in Basedow's photographs. He clearly wanted to document Aboriginal cultures as they had been in pre-contact times and occasionally went to some lengths to contrive such scenes. Active in Aboriginal affairs, he campaigned vigorously to improve Aboriginal people's living standards and gave popular public lectures on Aboriginal cultures and his travels.

In 1925 Basedow published his major anthropological work, *The Australian Aboriginal*, which brought together his observations on Aboriginal societies and was heavily illustrated with his own photographs.

The Museum acquired an extensive collection of Basedow's photographs when it became the custodian of the Australian Institute of Anatomy collection in 1984.

Herbert Basedow on Buxton, a riding camel, near present-day Granite Downs station, South Australia 1903
by Alfred Treloar using Basedow's camera

Men showing their scars, Port George IV, Western Australia 1916
by Herbert Basedow

WINNIE O'SULLIVAN'S LOCKET

This brass locket contains hidden treasures: a lock of hair and a small photograph. The grinning face in the photograph belongs to Les Darcy, champion boxer and Australian folk hero from East Maitland, New South Wales.

Of Irish Catholic descent, Les Darcy was born in 1895 and rose to boxing fame in the early years of the First World War. This success allowed him to build a house for his mother and to assist his poor family. In the heated atmosphere of Australia's conscription debates in 1916, Darcy slipped secretly away to America where he intended to make enough money from his boxing career to ensure his parents could live comfortably, and then to enlist for war service. Many in Australia, some in high places, accused him of cowardice, and in America he was unable to obtain fights that paid him well.

Unfortunately Darcy became ill following dental surgery he had had in Australia, and he died of septicaemia in Memphis in May 1917, aged 21. His sweetheart, Winnie O'Sullivan, was by his side.

Winnie and her brother Maurice both owned the locket at different times. Maurice, who had been a great mate of Les Darcy, carried the locket at the end of his watch chain for many years and would show it to anyone who asked. When he died the locket seems to have been passed to Winnie. It was found among her effects when she died in 1974, and was donated to the Museum through the Australian Government's Cultural Gifts Program in 2006.

Winnie O'Sullivan 1912

Winnie O'Sullivan's locket 1917

TRADE UNION BANNER

This 1920s Waterside Workers' Federation of Australia banner provided a graphic rallying point for the hundreds of Sydney wharf workers who belonged to one of the nation's oldest and most controversial unions.

The Waterside Workers' Federation of Australia was formed in 1902, built on a number of state-based unions, and amalgamated with the Seamen's Union of Australia in 1993.

The waterfront has been the site of many bitter industrial disputes. Prior to the Second World War, 'wharfies' were employed under the 'bull' system, where workers were selected for jobs on a daily basis. The work itself was backbreaking, cargoes being unloaded by hand with limited mechanical assistance.

The lack of secure employment, combined with dangerous and exhausting working conditions, encouraged militancy among the workforce. Throughout the union's history, a major theme has been the struggle to stop the use of a non-union workforce on the waterfront.

Donated to the Museum by the Sydney branch of the Waterside Workers' Federation, this banner consists of two large oil-painted canvases joined together with a cotton border. One side depicts a wharf scene with labourers hard at work unloading a ship. The reverse features a heroine wrapped in the Australian flag, with the dedication, 'In Memory of Our Fallen Members at the Front'.

Waterside Workers' Federation of Australia banner about 1920

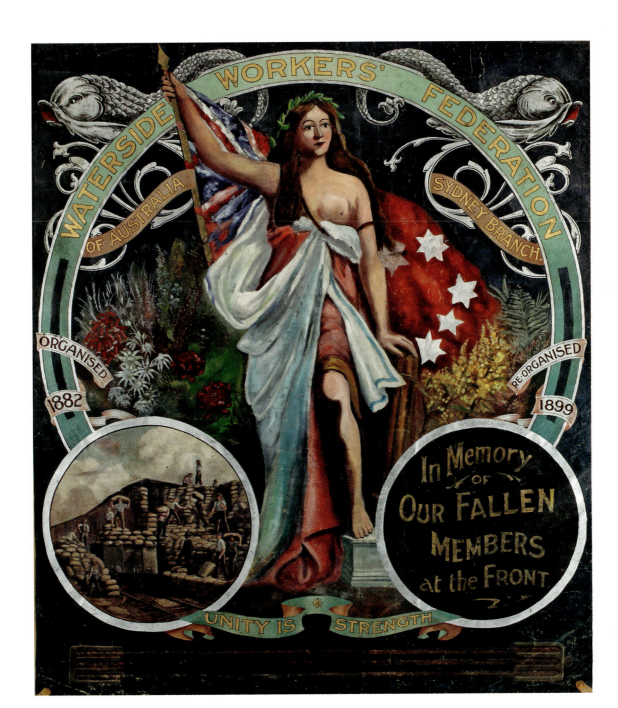

WESTWOOD'S
CITROËN MOTOR CAR

In 1925, this Citroën 5CV two-seat boat-tail tourer made history by being the first car to travel around Australia. The Citroën's owner and driver was Neville Westwood, a 22-year-old Seventh Day Adventist missionary. When Westwood bought the car in Perth, it had already travelled 48,000 kilometres.

Westwood left Perth with Greg Davies in the Citroën on 4 August 1925. Their adventures included passing the burnt wreckage of a car abandoned by adventurer Francis Birtles on an earlier trip to the Northern Territory. Along the way, they had to repair punctured tyres by filling them with grass and cowhide, and had to call on the help of local Aboriginal people to haul the car across the Fitzroy River.

Davies quit the journey at Albury on the border of New South Wales and Victoria, and Westwood continued alone to Melbourne and Adelaide. After travelling about 17,220 kilometres in 148 days, Westwood returned to Perth on 30 December 1925, escorted by a welcoming convoy of motorists.

Westwood kept the Citroën until his death in 1969, when it passed to his son Ron. In 1975, Ron Westwood began a restoration project on the Citroën, collecting spare parts, commissioning bodywork and rebuilding the engine, while retaining many original parts, including the radiator. Since purchasing the Citroën in 2005, the Museum has worked to preserve the car through extensive reconditioning work and periodic drives.

Westwood at the wheel of the Citroën in the Northern Territory 1925

Citroën 5CV with original licence plates and 1975 paintwork 1923

FRANCIS BIRTLES' BEAN MOTOR CAR

Almost 90 years ago, an Australian adventurer drove straight out of London and into the record books. Francis Birtles' journey in this Bean car is an extraordinary story of endurance by man and machine.

Between 1905 and his death in 1941, Birtles became known for his epic journeys across some of Australia's least mapped and most difficult terrain. Various companies, including Ford and Oldsmobile, commissioned Birtles to test the capacity of their new technologies in harsh and untried physical conditions.

Built by Bean Cars of Staffordshire, England, in 1925, this 14-horsepower, two-seater racing car was imported for promotional purposes by Bean's Australian agents, Barlow Motors of Melbourne. Nicknamed '*Sundowner*' due to Birtles' habit of turning up at rural homesteads just before suppertime, the car was of an innovative design, built for speed.

After establishing the fastest overland time between Darwin and Melbourne in 1926, Birtles became the first to drive the 26,000 kilometres overland from London to Melbourne in 1927–28. The nine-month trip was an extreme psychological and physical ordeal that covered Europe, the Middle East and South-East Asia to Singapore, and across Australia from Darwin to Melbourne.

Today the *Sundowner*'s battered, dented and scratched body still bears witness to its extraordinary journey across the world. Although now missing headlights, mudguards and bumper, it still appears much as it did upon arriving in Melbourne in 1928, right down to the traces of Middle Eastern sand and South-East Asian mud caked onto its underside.

The record-breaking *Sundowner* Bean car driven by Francis Birtles
1925

Francis Birtles 1920s

THYLACINE SKIN

This tanned skin of an adult thylacine, with the distinctive dark brown stripes of its species on its back, came from one of the last of the wild thylacines. It was caught by surveyor Charles Wilson in the Pieman River area of north-western Tasmania in 1930.

The Pieman River area is central to the history of the thylacine (also known as the 'Tasmanian tiger'). When in 1928 the Tasmanian Advisory Committee for Native Fauna recommended that the thylacine be protected, it was the area between the Arthur and Pieman rivers that was suggested as a potential reserve for thylacines. The last authenticated capture of a wild thylacine was in September 1930 at Mawbanna — also in north-west Tasmania.

Thylacines are now presumed to be extinct, although occasional unconfirmed sightings are still reported. A large carnivorous marsupial, the thylacine was not originally confined to the island-state of Tasmania. Fossilised remains of thylacines have been found in Victoria, South Australia, Western Australia and Queensland.

Believed to kill livestock, thylacines were often shot and trapped. Rural depression increased the pressure on the species — the thylacine was a convenient scapegoat for poor financial returns and high stock losses. Even when they were known to be close to extinction, little was done to save them. The thylacine was declared a protected species in July 1936, only a few weeks before the last thylacine died in Beaumaris Zoo, Hobart, on 7 September 1936.

Along with the thylacine skin, the Museum also holds what is believed to be the world's only wet specimen of a whole adult thylacine.

Skin of a thylacine shot in the Pieman River area of Tasmania 1930

'Native tiger shot by Weaver' 1869
Tasmanian Museum and Art Gallery

MILO DUNPHY'S PRAM

Myles Dunphy modified this pram so that he and his wife, Margaret, could take their baby son, Milo, on their bushwalks. An architect by profession, Myles was one of Australia's earliest campaigners for environmental conservation. Early in his life, Myles developed a love of the bush, especially the Blue Mountains. In 1914 he formed Sydney's first bushwalking club, the Mountain Trails Club, possibly the first group in Australia to combine bushwalking with wilderness conservation.

In 1931 Myles and Margaret pushed Milo in the pram from Oberon to Kanangra Tops in the Blue Mountains of New South Wales. Nicknamed the 'Kanangra Express', the pram could be folded up and carried over rugged terrain. That year, the Mountain Trails Club and other groups saved the Blue Gum Forest in the Blue Mountains. A year later, the National Parks and Primitive Areas Council was formed, with Dunphy as secretary. He campaigned to protect bushland and helped to change public attitudes of the bush as a place of exploitation to a place of recreation and appreciation.

The Blue Mountains National Park was formed in 1959, and the Kanangra Boyd National Park in the 1960s. Dunphy's maps of Kanangra and other areas became classics within the bushwalking fraternity and even assisted Lands Department draftsmen. Myles was awarded an Order of the British Empire for his services to conservation.

Milo followed in his father's footsteps and was a keen bushwalker and passionate wilderness campaigner. He donated the pram, as well as a large collection of bushwalking equipment, to the Museum in 1988.

The bush pram 'Kanangra Express' made by Myles Dunphy
about 1930

Myles Dunphy
about 1915
Colong Foundation

SOUTHERN CLOUD'S CLOCK

A five-shilling schoolyard sale resulted in the Museum acquiring a damaged clock from Australia's first major civil air disaster. The clock was salvaged from the wreck of the *Southern Cloud*, which crashed in the Snowy Mountains during bad weather on a Sydney to Melbourne flight in 1931.

Two crew and six passengers lost their lives in one of Australia's greatest aviation mysteries. Despite a comprehensive air search, the wreck lay undiscovered in the Snowy Mountains for 27 years.

The aircraft wreckage was found by accident more than 20 years later. On 26 October 1956 Tom Sonter, a worker on the Snowy Mountains Hydro-Electric Scheme, stumbled upon the wreck while bushwalking above the rugged Tooma River Gorge near Cabramurra. Within days, hundreds of people visited the site.

Many collected souvenirs, including schoolboy Alan Reid, who took the clock from the aircraft's instrument panel when he visited the wreck with his father, Alan, a former political journalist. In 1958 young Alan sold the battered clock components to John Boddington, of Dalton, near Goulburn. More than 75 years after the plane went down, Boddington donated the clock to the Museum.

The *Southern Cloud* tragedy played an important part in making air travel safer for Australians. After the *Southern Cloud* crash, it was recommended that radios be installed in all regular passenger planes, so weather forecasts could be conveyed to pilots while they were in the air.

Remnants of the *Southern Cloud*'s clock
1930

The crash site of the *Southern Cloud* 1958
National Library of Australia

Proclamation

In the name of His Majesty George the Fifth King of Great Britain, Ireland, and the British Dominions beyond the Seas, Emperor of India.

By Sir Douglas Mawson.

Whereas I have it in command from His Majesty King George the Fifth to assert the sovereign rights of His Majesty over British land discoveries met with in Antarctica. Now, therefore, I, Sir Douglas Mawson, do hereby proclaim and declare to all men that, from and after the date of these presents, the full sovereignty of the Territory of King George V Land and its extension under the name of Oates Land, situated between Longitudes 142 and 160 degrees east of Greenwich and between Latitude 66 degrees south and the South Pole. Included herein are the following Islands: Curzon Archipelago: Way Archipelago: Dixson Island: Mackellar Islets: Hodgeman Islets, vests in His Majesty King George the Fifth, his heirs and successors, for ever.

Given under my hand at Cape Denison on the Fifth day of January, 1931.

ANTARCTIC PROCLAMATION

Forty-six years after its burial beneath a cairn in Commonwealth Bay, members of the 1977 Australian Antarctic Expedition retrieved this proclamation, written in copperplate on rag paper by AL Kennedy, a physicist in Sir Douglas Mawson's Antarctic exploration party, and signed by Mawson on 5 January 1931.

The document, proclaiming British sovereignty over King George V Land (Antarctica) between longitudes 142 and 160 degrees east of Greenwich, and between latitude 66 degrees south and the South Pole, was found in a sealed canister made from three food tins that had been soldered together.

A distinguished polar explorer and scientist, Mawson led three research expeditions to Antarctica, the first from 1911 to 1914, and the second and third in 1929–30 and 1930–31. On instructions issued from Prime Minister Robert Bruce to Mawson on 12 September 1929, territorial acquisition (to 'plant the British flag') was to be the primary aim for Mawson's later voyages. However, his endeavour also achieved great advances in scientific exploration, oceanographic work and biological knowledge and sought to secure long-term prosperity for Australia.

Mawson's mapping of the Antarctic coastline became the basis for British claims for sovereignty over 5,800,000 square kilometres, or 42 per cent, of eastern Antarctic territory. This territory was later transferred from Britain to Australia under the *Australian Antarctic Territory Acceptance Act 1933*, which came into effect in 1936.

On its return to Australia in 1977 the proclamation was held by the Department of Home Affairs, then the National Library of Australia. It was transferred to the Museum's collection in 1993.

Antarctic proclamation
1931

The Antarctic proclamation canister made from food tins
1931

PHAR LAP'S HEART

Phar Lap's unusually large heart is one of the treasures of the Museum's collection, a testament to the great affection with which the horse is held by the Australian people.

An Australian sporting legend, Phar Lap's victory in the 1930 Melbourne Cup, in the midst of the Depression, elevated him to the status of national hero. Two years later Australia was stunned at the news of the horse's mysterious death in the United States. His heart was later found to weigh 6.35 kilograms, about 1.5 times larger than that of an average horse's heart, giving rise to the famous Australian saying 'a heart as big as Phar Lap's'.

A rich red chestnut gelding who stood 17 hands high, Phar Lap started his career as an outsider with neither the looks nor obvious racing potential of a future champion. He was leased cheaply by a relatively unknown trainer, Harry Telford. After failing to place in eight of his first nine starts, Phar Lap won 36 of his remaining 41 races, finishing unplaced only once — eighth in the 1931 Melbourne Cup while carrying a record weight of 68 kilograms. In his last start in North America's richest race, the Agua Caliente Handicap, Phar Lap came from last to win by three lengths in a race record time.

Phar Lap with jockey Jim Pike riding at Flemington race track
about 1930
State Library of Victoria

Phar Lap's heart 1932

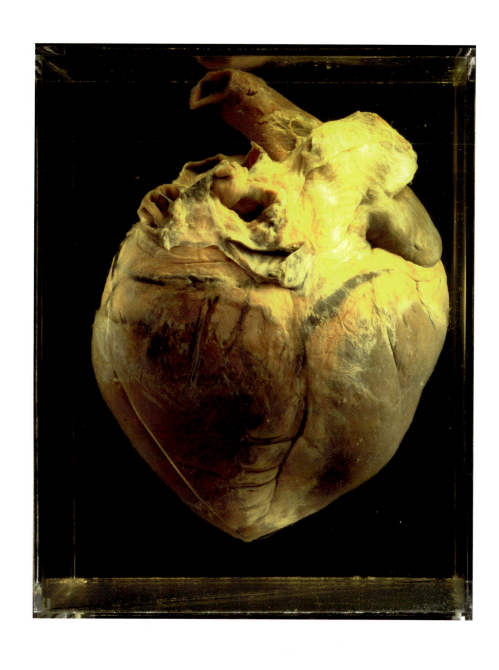

SAW DOCTOR'S WAGON

This wagon was workplace and home for Harold Wright and his family for over three decades. Wright, a young English carpenter, arrived in Melbourne at the height of the Depression. In 1935, he used the little money he had saved to convert a horse-drawn wagon into a combined workshop and home that he christened the *Road Urchin*.

For the next 34 years Wright, known as the 'Saw Doctor', travelled the length and breadth of eastern Australia, earning a vicarious living sharpening kitchen knives, saws and other tools. Along the way he met and married Dorothy Jean McDougall and together they raised a daughter, Evelyn May.

Initially pulled by a single horse, the wagon was then fitted to the chassis of a 1928 Chevrolet truck. Later it was towed by a 1948 David Brown tractor. Painted in bright colours and decorated with objects, toys and photographs, the *Road Urchin* was covered in signs, including 'The Sharpening King is Here'. It attracted a crowd wherever it went but brought little business. Nevertheless, Wright maintained a sanguine attitude to his life.

The Wright family, like thousands of others in the 1930s, took to the road to survive the Depression. Unlike most, however, they never did settle down and continued to travel until Wright's death in 1969. Following Wright's death, Dorothy sold the *Road Urchin* to a Wangaratta second-hand dealer. Peter and Wynn Herry bought the wagon and tractor in 1977 and kept it at their small farm until the Museum purchased it in 2002.

The *Road Urchin*, travelling home and workshop belonging to Harold Wright 1930s–60s

Harold Wright and his daughter, Evelyn 1956
by Jeff Carter

PERCIVAL GULL MONOPLANE

Born on 23 February 1897 in Albury, New South Wales, Edgar Wikner Percival was fascinated by flight from a young age. He studied engineering at Sydney Technical College and the University of Sydney, and served in the Royal Flying Corps during the First World War. After the war, Percival returned to Australia and started his own flight charter company while continuing to design aircraft.

In the 1930s, Percival moved to England and co-founded his own aircraft design company, the Percival Aircraft Company. He designed and manufactured the Percival Gull, a three-seater, low-wing monoplane in a number of variations that quickly established a reputation for high performance. In 1933, Charles Kingsford Smith broke the solo England to Australia record in his Gull Six *Miss Southern Cross*, and Jean Batten flew a Gull Six when she established world records between England and Brazil, Australia and New Zealand, and broke Kingsford Smith's England to Australia record in 1937.

During the Second World War, the Percival Aircraft Company developed a military version of the Gull, the Percival Proctor, as a training aircraft for the Royal Air Force. In 1944, Percival sold his interest in the company and moved to the United States.

The Museum's Gull Six monoplane, G-AERD, is one of the few surviving examples of Percival's most successful aircraft design. Manufactured in 1936 at Gravesend in Kent, England, it was sold to Ariane Dufau of Geneva, Switzerland, under the registration HB-OFU. After 40 years in Switzerland, the aircraft returned to England where it was restored and passed through a number of owners before the Museum purchased it in 1986.

Percival Gull monoplane with its English registration G-AERD 1936

Edgar Percival with his Mew Gull 15 March 1934

GUNA KINNE'S
LATVIAN FOLK COSTUME

Guna Kinne is a Latvian refugee who immigrated to Australia in 1948. Separated from her family, she escaped from her homeland using false documents. After living in various displaced persons camps in Germany, Kinne and her husband boarded the SS *Swalbard* to start a new life in Melbourne. Among her meagre belongings in a single suitcase was a Latvian folk costume. Kinne began making this costume in 1939 and continued to add to the ensemble until 1957.

The costume consists of eight separate pieces that, when combined, form an elegant outfit, rich in colours and textures. Kinne recalls she wore the costume a few times before she left Latvia, including at social occasions and as part of a folk dance troop. The first time she wore the costume after leaving Latvia was in Germany at a dance in December 1945, the night she met her husband.

Kinne's experiences are representative of post-war Latvian migration to Australia. After the Second World War, the Australian Government adopted a new immigration policy, which encouraged European emigration to Australia to boost population. By 1952, almost 20,000 Latvians had come to Australia as part of the program.

Many, including Kinne, participated in Latvian community organisations formed to help maintain cultural activities and provide mutual social support as emigrants adapted to life in their new country. Kinne and her husband became actively involved in the Good Neighbour Program and took part in various Latvian celebrations and gatherings where Kinne wore her traditional costume.

Guna Kinne wearing her costume outside her Wangaratta home 1955

Guna Kinne's Latvian folk costume, with felt crown 1939–57

HOLDEN PROTOTYPE NO. 1

Prototype no. 1 is the only survivor of three test Holden sedans built by hand in 1946 by American and Australian engineers at the General Motors workshop in Detroit. After extensive testing, the three prototypes of 'Australia's own car' were brought to Australia for road trials under local conditions.

The first Holden, the 48-215, rolled off the assembly line at Fishermen's Bend in Melbourne on 29 November 1948. Many saw the event as evidence of national maturity, proof that Australia had escaped its pastoral beginnings and embraced the modern industrial age.

Public reaction to the prospect of an Australian-built car had been extraordinary, with about 18,000 people signing up for a Holden without knowing a single detail about the car. By 1958 Holden sales accounted for more than 40 per cent of total car sales in Australia.

Following the public release of the Holden, General Motors-Holden's technicians fitted the no. 1 prototype with a new engine and sold it to Holden foreman Arthur Ling. The car was later traded to a Holden dealership in Morwell, Victoria, where it remained for 40 years, falling steadily into disrepair.

In 1999 Melbourne-based Holden enthusiasts Gavin and Graham Strongman purchased the car. They spent 12 months meticulously restoring the vehicle to its final pre-production form. Once restored, the prototype was purchased by Ian Metherall, who sold the car to the Museum in 2004.

The early Holdens have become complex symbols of freedom and independence, as well as suburban conformity, and are among the most recognisable cultural artefacts of 1950s Australia.

Holden prototype no. 1
1946

A designer at work on a clay model of the 'Australian car' 1946
GM Holden Ltd

JOHN MORIARTY'S BASKET

This traditional basket was made for John Moriarty by his mother Kathleen Murrmayibinya, and sent to him when he was living in St Francis House in Adelaide. Moriarty remembers how, aged just four, he was stolen from his school and from his Aboriginal mother: 'I tried to be a man but I remember crying and crying'. At least he knew that his mother was alive, and he was reunited with her ten years later.

Today Moriarty and his wife, Ros, manage the highly successful Balarinji Design company. A role model for young Aboriginal and Torres Strait Islander people, Moriarty is a successful businessman, a champion of Indigenous rights and a former soccer star. He describes himself as a 'Saltwater fella', identifying with his mother's people, the Yanyuwa, whose country lies around Borroloola in the Northern Territory. Named for his father John, he also identifies as a Moriarty (O'Muircheartaigh), one of the ancient Gaelic clans of County Kerry.

John's mother made this basket and sent it to him after he was taken from her, as a sign of her continuing love, and he has always treasured it. At their first reunion, when he was about 15, Moriarty says : 'My mother told me, in a very soft voice, "My son, you were going to school. I took you to school every day ... then I went to pick you up this day and you were gone"'.

John Moriarty as a small child with his mother Kathleen 1940s
courtesy John Moriarty

Small woven pandanus basket made by Kathleen Murrmayibinya about 1950

PROPERT CARAVAN

In 1950s Australia, the end of petrol rationing and post-Second World War prosperity led to increased car ownership and leisure time. Motoring and caravanning holidays became popular as an economical alternative to expensive rail travel and hotel accommodation. Keen competition between caravan manufacturers led to sleeker models with sophisticated interiors, boasting modern conveniences such as gas and electric refrigerators and ovens and electric lighting.

Thomas Propert founded the Propert Body Building Works in Sydney in 1910. For 20 years the company built car bodies for imported chassis but, partly in response to the economic downturn and changes to the car assembly industry, it moved into caravans in the 1930s.

Though locally manufactured Holdens were able to tow large caravans, the compact Propert caravan was designed to fill a niche in the new caravan market by enabling towing by less powerful, but more affordable, English and European sedans.

The pink Propert 'Trailaway' caravan was a one-off model, built by the company for advertising purposes in 1956. The van's fittings, which reflect contemporary trends in 1950s interior design, include a geometrically patterned linoleum floor, aluminium cookware, laminex bench tops, vinyl furniture coverings, Mexican-patterned curtains and a cream, red and black colour scheme.

Propert 'Trailaway' touring caravan 1956

ARTHUR STEWART'S GOLD NUGGET

This gold nugget was found near the Victorian town of Bealiba (70 kilometres west of Bendigo) on 26 June 1957 by Arthur Stewart, the owner of a small grazing property.

Stewart had stopped at the side of the road to repair the chain on his bicycle, which he was riding because his car had broken down six months earlier. His bad luck ended when he noticed gold glinting from a clod of earth next to the dirt road. He dug the 655-gram nugget out with his hands, then washed it in a nearby stream to confirm that he had discovered gold.

The next day Stewart formed a syndicate with mail contractor Gordon McDowell, farmer Tom Wright and his son of the same name. They called their syndicate 'Stewart's Surprise', took out miner's rights and pegged a claim around the spot where the nugget was found. The discovery caused a minor gold rush, with people hurrying in from surrounding areas.

On 1 July the *Sydney Morning Herald* reported that hundreds of people were fossicking around Bealiba with picks, shovels and pans.

Although the Victorian goldfields were famed for the gold nuggets they yielded, including some of the largest ever discovered, very few of these survive in their original form. This is because, soon after being found, nuggets were usually melted down. A few months after Stewart's chance discovery, the *Australian Amateur Mineralogist* bought his nugget. This magazine 'advocated for the retention of more of Australia's magnificent specimens for the sake of future generations'. The Museum purchased the nugget in 2011.

Gordon McDowell and Tom Wright, part of Arthur Stewart's syndicate, panning for gold 28 June 1957 photographer unknown

Gold nugget (shown actual size) discovered by Arthur Stewart 1957

JOHN KONRADS' MEDAL

At the 1960 Olympic Games in Rome, 18-year-old Australian swimmer John Konrads won this gold medal for the 1500-metre freestyle race. During the golden age of Australian swimming in the late 1950s and early 1960s, John and his younger sister Ilsa rewrote the swimming world record books.

After fleeing Latvia in the closing stages of the Second World War as Soviet forces moved west, the Konrads family arrived in Australia in 1949 as refugees. Facing the challenges of settling in a new country, John and Ilsa embraced swimming and, with the help of coach Don Talbot, began to set dozens of world records.

The teenage 'Konrads Kids' were at the forefront of a new era of Australian dominance over international swimming. In 1956, 14-year-old John was included as a team reserve for the Olympic Games in Melbourne, but the best was yet to come. At the 1960 Olympics he won three medals (including the gold and two bronze medals) of the 13 medals won by Australian swimmers.

In 2011, the Museum bid successfully at auction for a collection of medals, clothing and memorabilia belonging to John. This will allow the Museum to not only tell the story of John's incredible success in the pool, but also emphasise his achievements as a non-British migrant in 1950s and 1960s Australia.

Importantly, future displays of John's objects will also fulfil his wish to 'offer inspiration to the youth of today ... to show that a migrant kid can become a world beater'.

Olympic gold medal won by John Konrads
1960

Rome Olympics 1500m medalists (from left) Australians Murray Rose and John Konrads, and American George Breen
International Olympic Committee

ARTHUR STACE'S ETERNITY SIGN

The Eternity symbol has become an Australian icon. Behind it is the story of Arthur Stace, and his salvation in Sydney in the 1930s.

Stace was born in 1885, and he later recalled a childhood marred by hunger, neglect, and his parents' alcoholism. He served in France and England during the First World War but returned to Australia suffering from shell shock. Through the 1920s he was often out of work, broke and drunk.

In 1930, initially drawn by the promise of a hot cup of tea, Stace began to attend church regularly, and was able to give up alcohol. In 1932 at the Burton Street Baptist Tabernacle, Sydney, he heard the famous preacher John Ridley preach on the theme of 'Where will *you* spend Eternity?' With the word 'Eternity' ringing in his ears, Stace left the church and, finding some chalk in his pocket, knelt and wrote that word on the footpath.

He continued to chalk 'Eternity' on footpaths, walls and other surfaces across the city every day for the next 35 years until his death in 1967. By working in the early mornings he managed to keep his identity secret until 1956, when his story captured the imagination firstly of Sydney, and later the nation.

In the early 1960s Stace wrote 'Eternity' on some cardboard and gave it to a friend, Thelma Dodds. The Museum purchased it in 2000. It is one of only two surviving records of Stace's work, the other written on the inside of the bell in the GPO clock tower in Sydney.

'Eternity' written in chalk on cardboard by Arthur Stace 1960s

Eccentric Sydney identity Arthur Stace
3 July 1963
by Trevor Dallen
Fairfax Syndication

FAITH BANDLER'S GLOVES

Civil rights campaigner Faith Bandler wore these gloves while lobbying for the 'Yes' case for the 1967 Referendum, which addressed the discrimination against Aboriginal people written into the Australian Constitution. Bandler recalled wearing her white gloves when addressing predominantly white female audiences during the campaign.

Bandler was one of a dedicated group of Australians, Indigenous and non-Indigenous, who campaigned for the 'Yes' case. The referendum was one of the few successful in Australian history and remains the highest 'Yes' vote in an Australian referendum. It achieved the inclusion of Aboriginal people in the census and allowed the Australian Goverment to make laws for Aboriginal people, and it also retains a wider symbolic significance.

Born in 1920 in northern New South Wales to an Islander family, Bandler's activism was influenced by her father's experience of forcible relocation from the Pacific island of Ambryn to work the sugar cane plantations. In 1952 she married Hans Bandler, a Jewish refugee from Vienna.

During the 1950s and 1960s, Bandler became involved in the campaign for Aboriginal rights, encouraged by fellow activists Pearl Gibbs and Lady Jessie Street. Bandler was a highly successful campaigner and became a prominent public figure. In the 1970s she turned her attention to writing and to the struggle to achieve legal recognition of Australia's Islander peoples. She was awarded the Medal of the Order of Australia in 1984 and was made a Companion in the Order of Australia in 2009. Bandler donated the gloves to the Museum in 1998.

Faith Bandler at Sydney Town Hall 27 May 1967
by George Lipman
Fairfax Syndication

Faith Bandler's gloves
1960s

JACK WHERRA'S BOAB NUT

Kimberley artist and Ngarinyin man Jack Wherra began carving boab nuts while serving an 18-year sentence at Broome Regional Prison in Western Australia. Jack Wherra's story, as a tribal man who found himself at the mercy of both white and black law after a tribal incident, provides insights into the complexities of contact history.

Made between 1964 and 1966, the boab nuts are carved with rows of scenes in a series of frames, inspired by the comic strips Wherra used to read in jail. The narratives contain images of people and events in the Kimberley landscape and provide a significant social record of cross-cultural relations between Aboriginal and non-Aboriginal people.

Probably used as gifts and exchange items before European settlement, boab nut carving is an art form unique to the Kimberley.

Attempt to Seduce a Wife 1960s
by Jack Wherra

Boab nut carver (believed to be Jack Wherra) 1979
National Archives of Australia

AURUKUN WALLABY SCULPTURE

George Ngallametta, with MacNaught and Joe Ngallametta, created *Pun'ka* (Wallaby) in 1962 for a series of ceremonial dances at Aurukun Mission in Queensland at the request of Reverend William Mackenzie, who was approaching retirement. The sculpture was used to lead a ceremonial dance that enacted the fight between two wallabies during the Dreaming, through which the species was spread over the land.

Anthropologist Frederick McCarthy from the Australian Institute of Aboriginal Studies filmed the ceremonies and collected this and other sculptures as part of the process of documenting five significant Wik dances. Purchased by the Museum in the 1970s, the forelimbs and tail of the wooden sculpture are carved in one piece, while the ears and hind limbs have been carved separately and attached.

In 1988, the Aurukun sculptures were displayed in New York as part of the first major exhibition of Aboriginal art overseas, *Dreamings: The Art of Aboriginal Australia*. The exhibition drew large crowds and by the time it had travelled to Chicago and Los Angeles, it had attracted over half a million visitors.

Dreamings changed how people, both in Australia and overseas, viewed Aboriginal art. Art critics in particular, began thinking about Aboriginal art not as ethnographic objects made by a 'primitive people' but as examples of fine art.

Pun'ka **(Wallaby)** 1962 by George Ngallametta with MacNaught and Joe Ngallametta, Thawungadha, western Cape York Peninsula

YIRRKALA BARK PETITION

The 1963 Yirrkala bark petition has become a symbolic marker of Aboriginal protest. Yet few realise that the Yolngu people produced four bark petitions and a series of four paper petitions at this time, which they presented to the Australian parliament and to non-Indigenous activists of the Federal Council for the Advancement of Aboriginal and Torres Strait Islanders.

Each of the bark petitions is unique and features traditional designs and motifs. These petitions expressed concern about the Australian Government's excision of 300 square kilometres of land in the Gove Peninsula of the Northern Territory for a bauxite mine, and called for Indigenous land rights to be recognised.

During the 1960s, Yolngu artists began using their art to campaign for land rights. The public display of their images, previously reserved for ceremonial use, was a powerful statement of Yolngu people's continuous relationship with, and ownership of, their land.

There is a long history of Aboriginal people petitioning government and colonial authorities. These Yirrkala bark petitions, however, were the first to combine Indigenous visual imagery and language with the traditional British form of a written petition.

Although these petitions did not stop the mine at Gove, they led the Australian Government to appoint a select committee to hear their concerns. Ultimately, the petitions resulted in the passing of the *Northern Territory Land Rights Act 1976*.

The petition held by the Museum was presented to Gordon Bryant, activist and parliamentary member for Wills. After his death, Bryant's family chose to donate the bark to the safekeeping of the Museum.

One of four Yirrkala bark petitions prepared by the Yolngu Elders
1963

Galarrwuy Yunupingu looking at Yirrkala bark petitions on land rights presented to the Australian Parliament with Aboriginal Affairs Minister Mr Ian Viner
1977
National Archives of Australia

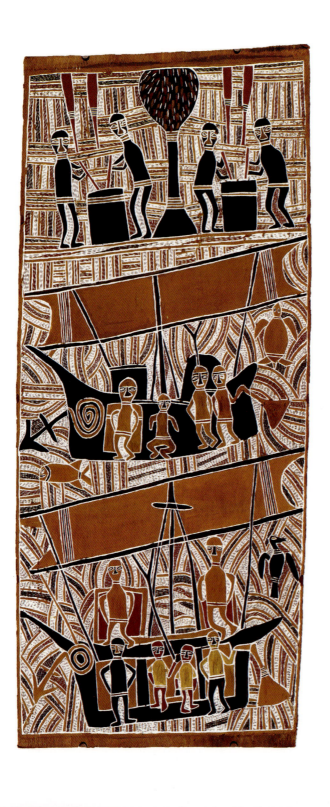

MATHAMAN MARIKA'S BARK PAINTING

Mathaman Marika was from the Rirratjingu clan of the Yolngu people, living at Yirrkala in eastern Arnhem Land. He was a passionate advocate of Indigenous rights and an accomplished artist, who was most prolific from the late 1950s until his death in 1970.

This untitled painting depicts a Macassan *prau* (sailing boat) with sailors and a boat with a tripod mast, and is unusual in that it also details a trepang (sea cucumber) processing site, showing Aboriginal men boiling the trepang in large metal cauldrons under a tamarind tree.

During his artistic career, Marika developed his own particular style for painting the travels of the Djang'kawu ancestral beings to Yalangbara, the Morning Star ceremony, and stories from the nearby community of Nhulunbuy, such as that of Wuyal the Sugarbag Spirit.

He also regularly painted the Wagilag Sisters, associated with the site of Marwuyu in central Arnhem Land. The rights to paint this were apparently established early in the twentieth century by Marika's grandfather during an exchange of ceremonial songs and paintings with the Manhdalpuy clan.

Untitled bark painting
1964
by Mathaman Marika

Mathaman Marika at Yirrkala 1959

NARRITJIN MAYMURU'S CREATION STORY

Narritjin Maymuru was born in Yolngu country to the north of Blue Mud Bay in eastern Arnhem Land. He and his family spent most of their lives at Yirrkala mission. In 1974 the family moved 200 kilometres south to their own clan land at Djarrakpi, where they produced bark paintings and craftwork to sell at Yirrkala. As well as earning money from the sale of paintings, Narritjin used bark paintings to teach his children about their clan land and its ancestral history, and to teach anthropologists and filmmakers about Yolngu society.

Creation Stories of the Manggalili Clan depicts the ancestrally created Manggalili lands using ochres on bark. The painting is divided into sections, with a divided central column containing humans, a fish, a crocodile and stars and a black bird. Arranged on either side are scenes depicting sea and land creatures, and humans performing a variety of activities. Much of the background is decorated in slightly wavy bands of *rarrk* (cross-hatching) on coloured dashes.

The middle of the painting represents the natural processes involved in removing the dead from the world of the living. It also expresses the idea that from death comes new life. The lower half of the painting represents the death of the ancestor 'Guwak' and the ascent of the spirits to the Milky Way.

Narritjin was an inventive and prolific artist and the Museum holds a large number of his works in its collection.

Creation Stories of the Manggalili Clan about 1965
by Narritjin Maymuru

EXPO MARK II SOUND CHAIR

The Expo Mark II sound chair is an enduring legacy of Australia's contribution to the 1967 International and Universal Exposition (Expo 67) in Montreal, Canada.

Visited by 20 million people, the glass-walled Australian pavilion developed by the Australian Government covered 2700 square metres: a haven of space and tranquillity floating above a bushland setting. Inside, 240 innovative sound chairs offered foot-weary Expo visitors the chance to listen to information about Australia while they sat in comfort.

Robin Boyd, who designed the Australian pavilion's interior and displays, commissioned Melbourne-based contemporary furniture designers Grant and Mary Featherston to develop a 'talking chair'. The chairs were moulded from a single piece of polystyrene in a continuous circular form. Green or orange cushions indicated if the audio was English or French. The speakers installed in the headrests were activated by the pressure of a person sitting in the chair. The audio system, which cost one million dollars to produce, played three-minute segments of famous Australians talking about the exhibits surrounding the visitor, including models of Canberra, the Parkes radio telescope, the Snowy Mountains Hydro-Electric Scheme and a display of Australia's new decimal currency.

The Expo 67 sound chair was so popular with the public that it was adapted for the domestic market from the original chair design, with built-in speakers and volume control. The Mark II sound chair purchased by the Museum in 2007 was produced between 1967 and 1970.

Hostess Hedy Glesinger on an original sound chair in the distinctive Australian pavilion at Expo 67 in Montreal
National Archives of Australia

The Expo Mark II sound chair

PLAY SCHOOL ROCKET CLOCK

The *Play School* television program produced by the Australian Broadcasting Commission (ABC) holds a significant place in the imagination and memory of generations of Australians. The props used on the set of *Play School*, like the toys that regularly appear on the show, are instantly recognisable to viewers past and present. One of the best loved of these is undoubtedly the rocket clock.

The ABC transmitted the first episode of *Play School* in 1966, basing it on the format of the BBC production of the same name, which had begun in 1964. For the first series, the set for the Australian show was copied from the British set, but it was soon revised and rebuilt. The new sets included three 'magic windows' and the 'flower clock' used to accompany storytelling. After the introduction of colour TV in 1975, the set was rejigged again and the 'rocket clock' added. Each day one of the clocks, with its own particular theme music, would rotate to reveal a diorama that acted as a visual cue for that episode's story. These props were a key part of the *Play School* set until a major redesign in 1999.

Play School has been a cornerstone of children's television for over three decades and has become a true icon of Australian television history. The program still screens each day and continues to attract new fans as the next generation of Australian viewers are encouraged to wonder, think, feel and imagine.

Actors George Spartels and Benita Collings in ABC TV show *Playschool*
Newspix/News Limited

***Play School* rocket clock**
1976

AZARIA CHAMBERLAIN'S BLACK DRESS

The disappearance of two-month-old Azaria Chantel Loren Chamberlain on 17 August 1980 is one of the most infamous events in contemporary Australian history. The explanation of her disappearance, that she was prey to a dingo on a family holiday to Ayers Rock (now Uluru), was a subject of intense public speculation. Rumours flew about her parents, Michael and Lindy Chamberlain, and their religious beliefs. This tiny black dress caused outrage as it was seen as 'unnatural' to dress a baby in black.

An initial inquest agreed with the Chamberlains' statement that a dingo had entered the tent and taken the baby, but a subsequent trial found Lindy Chamberlain guilty of murder. Lindy was imprisoned for three years before a royal commission cleared both her and Michael of any connection with the disappearance of their daughter.

During the 1980s, the subject of the guilt or innocence of Lindy Chamberlain obsessed the nation. Discussions rarely focused on the facts of the case. Out of this frenzy of speculation the rumour emerged that Lindy Chamberlain always dressed her baby in black. A one-off creation that Lindy originally made for her son, Reagan, to match one of her own outfits, the dress became yet another sign of apparent guilt to an insatiable public.

Controversy and interest in the Chamberlain case continues today. On 12 June 2012 a fourth coronial inquest found that Azaria died as a result of being attacked and taken by a dingo, and ordered that Azaria's death certificate be amended immediately.

Azaria Chamberlain's black dress, panties and booties 1980

UTA UTA TJANGALA'S PAINTING

The remote Northern Territory settlement of Papunya has been heralded as the birthplace of contemporary Aboriginal art. In 1971 a group of Aboriginal men, with the assistance of school teacher Geoffrey Bardon, began to produce acrylic paintings. Bardon encouraged the senior men of the various language groups living at Papunya to develop ways of adapting their traditional art to Western materials.

Papunya artists experimented with colour and style to tell their Dreaming stories linked to land, history and culture. These artists formed one of the most successful Indigenous arts cooperatives, Papunya Tula Artists, which still operates today.

Uta Uta (Wuta Wuta) Tjangala was conceived at the claypan site of Ngurrapalangu, near the border of the Northern Territory and Western Australia. This acrylic painting depicts Tjangala's Dreaming ancestor Tjuntamurtu, who inhabits a cave at Ngurrapalangu, as the central figure, with several other Dreamings that pass through the artist's country. The painting's title, *Yumari*, means 'mother-in-law', and refers to the rock hole where the Yina (Old Man) finally came to rest after an illicit liaison with his mother-in-law.

Tjangala was a Pintupi man and one of the original group of Papunya artists. In 1981, the *Yumari* canvas played a role in the Pintupi's preparations to return to their homelands. As Pintupi men sat around the canvas on the outskirts of Papunya, helping Tjangala with his painting, they talked about setting up a community on their own land at Kintore, 280 kilometres to the west. They left for Kintore a few months later. Tjangala continued to paint the sites of Ngurrapalangu and Yumari until the late 1980s.

Tim Payungka Tjapangarti, Yumpuluru Tjungurrayi and Uta Uta Tjangala working on *Yumari* 1981
by Fred Myers

Yumari 1981
by Uta Uta Tjangala
© estate of the artist 2012 licensed by Aboriginal Artists Agency

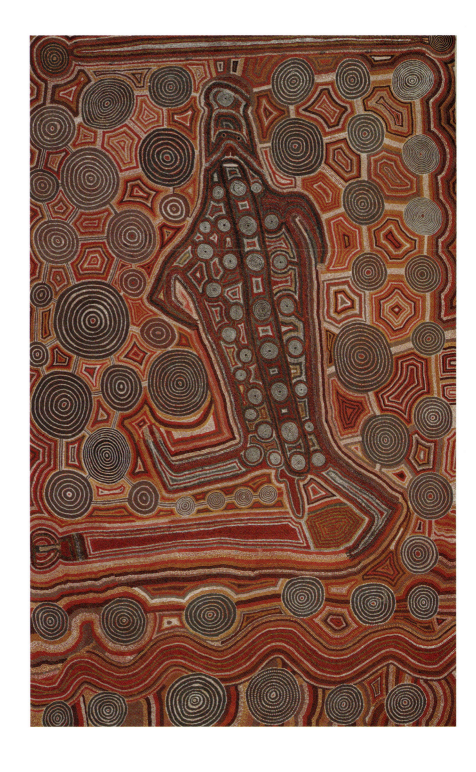

ĐÀN TRE

Minh Tam Nguyen was born in Bình Định province of central Vietnam in 1947. As a teenager training to be a priest with the Redemptorists, he studied music until poor health forced him to leave the order. In 1968 with his country at war, Nguyen enlisted in the Army of the Republic of Vietnam (South Vietnamese Army).

From 1975 Nguyen spent six years as a prisoner of war in the 're-education' camps of the People's Liberation Armed Forces, or Vietcong, in central Vietnam. During breaks from hard labour, and using whatever materials were to hand, Nguyen invented and played a musical instrument that combined features from Vietnamese bamboo zithers and Western instruments like the guitar. As Nguyen attempted to improve the sound quality and range of the instrument, it evolved from 18, to 21, and then finally 23 strings. He called it the *Đàn Tre*, which means 'bamboo musical instrument'.

Nguyen made this 23-stringed *Đàn Tre* in a Philippine refugee camp after fleeing Vietnam in 1981. He brought the instrument with him when he and his son came to Australia in 1982. Playing the *Đàn Tre* connected him to the family he had been forced to leave behind in Vietnam.

In 1990, Nguyen was at last reunited with his mother, wife and other children through the Family Migration Program, after the Vietnamese Government began issuing exit visas. Later that year, Nguyen donated the *Đàn Tre* to the Museum.

Đàn Tre, an original creation by Minh Tam Nguyen 1981

Nguyen with his *Đàn Tre* in Sydney about 1990
courtesy Minh Tam Nguyen

PEACE BUS

This Leyland Atlantean double-decker bus, known as the 'Peace Bus', was driven around eastern Australia to promote world peace and nuclear disarmament.

Purchased in 1982 by the People for Nuclear Disarmament from the New South Wales Urban Transport Authority, the bus operated as a mobile peace education centre. Between 1984 and 1987 it travelled over 24,000 kilometres throughout New South Wales, Victoria, South Australia, Queensland and the Australian Capital Territory, and was visited by more than 40,000 people.

The mural, designed by artist Jenny Short and painted by a team of 90 volunteers, features images of Australian and Pacific flora and fauna, and peace motifs. This reflects the concern of the People for Nuclear Disarmament for the environmental and social implications of nuclear weapons testing and warfare.

Leyland Atlantean double-decker bus, known as the 'Peace Bus' 1984

HARVEST OF ENDURANCE SCROLL

Harvest of Endurance is a 50-metre-long scroll that represents two centuries of Chinese contact with, and emigration to, Australia. Stories of hardship and survival, resourcefulness and reward are painted in the traditional *gong bi* (meaning 'meticulous brushwork') style.

Artist Mo Xiangyi, assisted by Wang Jingwen, painted the scroll and Mo Yimei carried out the historical research. Sponsored by the Australia–China Friendship Society in celebration of the Australian Bicentenary in 1988, the scroll took just over 12 months to complete and consists of 18 elaborately painted panels.

Painted with ink and colour, the detailed images depict Chinese Australians engaged in agriculture, mining, construction and commerce, and in social, political and religious activities. This section of the scroll shows the hardships endured by Chinese labourers before the 1850s. On the right, labourers in search of work walk along a winding country road past bullock teams. On the left, Chinese workers clear bushland.

The *gong bi* style of painting is defined both by the methodology used to apply colour and ink and the painter's philosophical approach to the subject matter. The aim is to achieve harmony through balance and the principles of yin and yang. Thick lines are balanced with fine lines; soft colours are contrasted with more vibrant colours.

This magnificant work highlights the contribution of Australian Chinese to the development of Australia, an often unacknowledged part of our history.

Harvest of Endurance scroll 1988
Australia–China Friendship Society

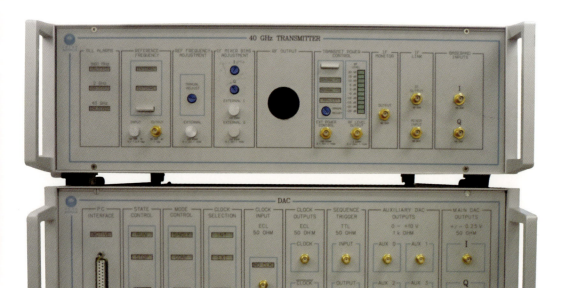

CSIRO WLAN TEST-BED

During the early 1990s, researchers at the Commonwealth Scientific and Industrial Research Organisation (CSIRO) developed a new approach to wireless data transmission. CSIRO's wireless local area network (WLAN) solved the main problem of indoor wireless networking — radio waves bouncing off walls and furniture, creating reverberation and an echo that distorts the signal. This invention laid the foundation for wi-fi, the high-speed wireless networking technology used to connect billions of phones, tablets, computers, printers, routers, televisions, cameras and games consoles.

The WLAN project started in CSIRO's Radiophysics division (now the CSIRO ICT Centre). As part of their work in radioastronomy, the division developed a Fast Fourier Transform (FFT) chip to encode and decode data streams rapidly. The mathematical functions performed by the FFT chip are at the heart of CSIRO's WLAN invention.

On 23 November 1992, CSIRO filed for a patent with the United States Patent and Trademark Office. Patent no. 5,487,069 listed five CSIRO scientists as the inventors: John O'Sullivan, Graham Daniels, Terence Percival, Diethelm Ostry and John Deane. The invention suffered from widespread patent infringement and, in April 2012, CSIRO negotiated a major settlement with the world's leading computer manufacturers. The Wireless LAN team won the 'non-European' category of the 2012 European Inventors Award, the first Australian researchers to win this prestigious honour.

In 2011, CSIRO donated to the Museum the four main hardware components used in the original WLAN prototype test-bed, as well as other devices used during the WLAN project.

Digital to analogue converter (top) and 40 GHz transmitter unit from original CSIRO WLAN test-bed
CSIRO

RON MUNCASTER'S PLATFORM SHOE

This buckled, sling-back platform shoe with peek-a-boo toe was part of the Lucille Balls costume made by Ron Muncaster, which won the First Single Excellent Prize in the 1994 Mardi Gras costume competition.

The Sydney Gay and Lesbian Mardi Gras is an event of cultural and social importance. It attracts popular interest, media coverage, a large local audience and overseas visitors to Sydney every year. Muncaster is a well-known costume designer and remains one of the most successful within the context of Mardi Gras. He has been awarded more prizes for his costumes than any other designer in the history of the competition.

'It's amazing how Sydney has taken Mardi Gras to its heart,' said Muncaster. 'I am always overwhelmed when I walk up Oxford Street and reach Taylor Square to hear the cheers from the crowd and see the smiling faces.

That's the reward for all the worry and work I put into my costumes. I was very flattered to be named Queen of Mardi Gras, but I get embarrassed when people curtsy to me.'

Spray-painted silver, the shoes are covered in triangles of metallic silver plastic tape, with pink, green, turquoise and blue sequins. The Lucille Balls costume, composed of a skirt made from fibreglass rods and styrofoam balls, fishnet singlet and stockings, collar, headdress, belt, shoes, armbands and rings, was made for and worn by Muncaster's late partner, Jacques Straetmans.

The entire costume, including the shoes, were donated to the Museum by Muncaster in 2005.

Jacques Straetmans in the Lucille Balls Mardi Gras costume 1994
courtesy Ron Muncaster

Buckled sling-back platform shoe with peek-a-boo toe 1994

NGURRARA I

Ngurrara I is a huge collaborative painting depicting the country of Walmajarri and Wangkajunga peoples of the Great Sandy Desert. A team of 19 traditional owners painted the canvas as evidence to be offered in the Ngurrara Native Title application, a claim for 800,000 hectares of land that was due to be considered by the National Native Title Tribunal the following year.

A multi-coloured acrylic painting on canvas, depicting an aerial view map of the artists' country, the artwork is divided into two sections by a black line, representing the Canning Stock Route, and features circular designs and a white snake in one corner, which are set against a predominantly red background.

As one of the senior artists, Peter Skipper, explains, 'The stories and the bodies of our old people are in their country, our country.

We wanted to make *kartiya* [white people] understand our ownership of our country'.

After completing *Ngurrara I*, the artists decided to recreate it with some changes that would improve the chances of their native title claim succeeding in the High Court. It was this second *Ngurrara* canvas, produced in 1997, that was eventually used in the hearings. It proved to be an effective strategy: the claim was decided in favour of the traditional owners in 2007.

The second canvas remains in the possession of the community while the first was purchased by the Museum in 2010, as an important document of the strength of Aboriginal attachment to land in the Great Sandy Desert.

Ngurrara I 1996
by Ngurrara artists and claimants

Conservation and Registration staff rolling out *Ngurrara Canvas I* at the Museum

KEN THAIDAY'S TRIPLE BEIZAM HEADDRESS

Made by Torres Strait Islander artist Ken Thaiday Senior, this hammerhead shark (*beizam*) headdress is worn on a dancer's head. It is made up of several moveable parts, and the wearer manipulates the headdress by pulling a series of strings.

The *beizam* headdress is specific to the mythologies and religious traditions of Thaiday's clan and island group. Born on Erub (Darnley Island) in 1950, Thaiday learned the importance of art and dance from his father. Prior to becoming a full-time artist, he worked as a dancer and, in 1987, he began constructing dance artefacts for his Cairns-based Torres Strait Islander dance troupe.

Employing non-traditional materials and construction styles, his works have evolved over time into elaborately articulated headdresses known as 'dance machines'. Thaiday's *beizam* headdresses epitomise his practice of combining traditional and contemporary forms.

Triple *beizam* headdress with reef fish 1999
by Ken Thaiday Senior

TRISTAN YOUNG'S BUSH TOYS

The Museum's collection of bush toys contains 68 objects created between 1997 and 1999 by 11 emerging and established artists from three Eastern Arrernte communities in Central Australia. They made the figures from found and salvaged materials, such as coiled wire and fabric, as a craft activity and to provide toys for children.

Aboriginal communities have traditionally produced toys for their children as teaching tools to prepare them for adulthood. Historically these were miniature versions of implements and utensils that were essential for daily survival, such as spears, shields and boomerangs. Since the introduction of new materials like metal, plastic and glass, these toys have evolved to reflect the environment and lifestyle of the makers.

When many Aboriginal people became involved in working on cattle stations in the 1960s, toys were modelled on horses and riders, or incorporated scenes of stockmen, stockyards and rodeos. Over time, toys were modelled on changing technology in use on cattle stations, including trucks, motorbikes, helicopters and fixed-wing aircraft.

Horse and Cowboy 1999
by Tristan Young

AUSTRALIAN FLAG FROM THE THE WORLD TRADE CENTER

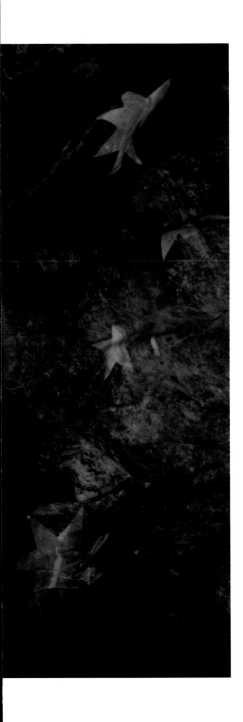

At 8.45 am on 11 September 2001, a passenger plane, which had been hijacked by Al Qaeda terrorists, crashed into the North Tower of New York's World Trade Center. Fifteen minutes later, a second plane slammed into the South Tower. By 10.30 am the Twin Towers had collapsed, removing one of the city's most famous landmarks, and killing more than 2600 people, including ten Australians.

In the aftermath of this destruction, thousands of objects were recovered from the World Trade Center site. Among these was an Australian flag. The 120- by 178-centimetre flag was intact but heavily soiled and crumpled. It was found in the basement of World Trade Center Three, which had been destroyed by falling debris from the collapse of the Twin Towers.

The flag is believed to have been used for ceremonial purposes in World Trade Center Three's 22-storey Marriott Hotel, which once stood on the plaza between the towers. New York Police Department Emergency Services Unit Detective, Patrick McGee, presented the flag to Australia's Consul-General, Ken Allen, in a private ceremony in August 2004. Since its arrival in Australia, the flag has regularly been displayed at the Museum during September, to commemorate those Australians whose lives were lost in the terrorist attacks.

Australian flag recovered from the ruins of the World Trade Center 2001

DULCIE GREENO'S NECKLACE

Shell necklace-making is the most significant cultural tradition of Tasmanian Aboriginal women. Dating back at least 2600 years, it is also one of the few traditions that has continued without interruption since the European colonisation of Tasmania in 1803.

This necklace was made by Dulcie Greeno, an elder of the Tasmanian Aboriginal community. She was born in 1923 on Cape Barren Island, one of the Furneaux Islands group. She lived for many years on nearby Flinders Island, where she and her family continued the Aboriginal traditions of mutton-birding and crayfishing, and now lives in Launceston.

Greeno has been making necklaces for more than 40 years, but first began practising as a child. Shell-stringing is a painstaking process, requiring great skill and patience. Some of Greeno's necklaces use as many as 1700 shells, including rice shells so small they can fit under a fingernail.

Shell necklaces were originally made as adornment for ceremonies, as gifts, and as objects to be traded with other sea and land peoples for ochre and stone tools. After European colonisation, necklaces were also sold or exchanged for food, clothing and other essential supplies.

The knowledge and skills of shell processing and stringing has been passed down through generations of women, and is an opportunity for women of all ages to come together and share stories, pass knowledge to younger generations and continue to affirm their culture.

Lola Greeno, Dulcie Greeno and Julie Gough on a beach near Devonport, Tasmania
2005

Shell necklace of rice shells, white toothies and green maireeners
2003
by Dulcie Greeno

ESME TIMBERY'S SHELLWORK

For more than a hundred years, the Aboriginal women of La Perouse, Sydney, have been producing artworks elaborately decorated with shells. This shellwork Sydney Harbour Bridge was made by Bidjigal woman Esme Timbery. Born in 1931, Timbery comes from a family of noted shellworkers. She learnt her techniques and designs from her mother, Elizabeth. As a child and young woman, Timbery collected shells with members of her family on the shores of Botany Bay and Cronulla, in Sydney's south and on the south coast of New South Wales.

Timbery's great grandmother, 'Queen' Emma Timbery was a noted shellworker. Her wares were regularly shown and sold at the Sydney Royal Easter Show, and travelled to England as part of an exhibition of Australian crafts in 1910.

The production of shellwork artefacts dates to at least the late 19th century, with documents recording women selling shell baskets at Circular Quay and Botany Bay in the 1880s. The shellwork tradition has transformed over many decades. It began as an Aboriginal women's craftwork, was adapted and tailored to suit the tourist souvenir market, and some works are now considered high art.

Esme Timbery is one of only a few La Perouse Aboriginal women making shellwork today. Her pieces are highly prized, and are held in museums and art galleries around Australia. In 2005 Timbery won the inaugural Parliament of New South Wales Indigenous Art Prize for one of her Harbour Bridge works, constructed from a plywood skeleton covered in fabric, glitter and shellwork.

Shellwork Sydney Harbour Bridge 2006
by Esme Timbery
VISCOPY

LIST OF OBJECTS

LIST OF OBJECTS

13. John Gore's telescope, 1760s. Donated by Jack Gallaway in 2006.

14. James Cook's bust, about 1788. Purchased by the Museum in 2007.

16. Sir Andrew Snape Hamond's table, 1790s. Purchased in 2006.

19. Governor King's snuffbox, 1801. Purchased in 2006.

20. The *Investigator*'s stream anchor, 1801. Transferred from the Department of Transport in 1981.

23. George Ranken's landau, 1821. Purchased in 1980.

24. Convict-era shirt and punishment shoe, about 1830. Purchased in 2005.

27. Thomas Alsop's convict love token, 1833. Purchased in 2008.

28. Batman land deed, 1835. Purchased in 1997.

30. Leichhardt nameplate, 1848. Purchased in 2006.

32. Major Sir Thomas Mitchell's duelling pistols, used in 1851. Purchased in 1983.

35. Robert O'Hara Burke's water bottle, about 1860. Purchased in 2005.

36. Tim Whiffler's Melbourne Cup, 1867. Purchased in 2011.

39. Paddle Steamer *Enterprise*, 1878. Purchased in 1984.

40. Ned Kelly's Jerilderie letter, 1879. Purchased in 2001.

43. Nelson's dog collar, 1881. Purchased in 2011.

44. Miss Faithfull's wool dress, about 1885. Donated through the Australian Government's Cultural Gifts Program by James IF Maple-Brown, Diana Boyd and Pamela Maple-Brown in 2005.

47. Kimberley points. Transferred from the Australian Institute of Anatomy Collection in 1984.

48. William Barak's illuminated address, 1886. Purchased in 2008.

51. Budd Billy's breastplate, about 1896. Transferred from Australian Institute of Anatomy Collection in 1984.

53. Klondike flag, 1898. Purchased in 2011.

54. Oscar's sketchbook, about 1899. Transferred from Australian Institute of Anatomy Collection in 1984.

56. Dally Messenger's representative cap, 1907. Purchased in 2007.

59. Sunshine harvester, 1911. Purchased in 1992.

60. Herbert Basedow's photograph, 1916. Transferred from Australian Institute of Anatomy Collection in 1984.

63. Winnie O'Sullivan's locket, 1917. Donated through the Australian Government's Cultural Gifts Program in 2006.

64. Trade union banner, about 1920. Donated to the Museum by the Sydney branch of the Waterside Workers' Federation in 1985.

66. Westwood's Citroën motor car, 1923. Purchased in 2005.

69. Francis Birtles' Bean motor car, 1925. Donated to the Australian government in 1929.

70. Thylacine skin, 1930. Purchased in 1999.

73. Milo Dunphy's pram, about 1930. Donated by Milo Dunphy in 1988.

74. *Southern Cloud*'s clock, 1930. Donated by John Boddington in 2006.

77. Antarctic proclamation, 1931. Transferred from the National Library of Australia in 1993.
78. Phar Lap's heart, 1932. Transferred from the Australian Institute of Anatomy Collection in 1984.
80. Saw Doctor's wagon, 1930s–60s. Purchased in 2002.
82. Percival Gull monoplane, 1936. Purchased in 1986.
85. Guna Kinne's Latvian folk costume, 1939–57. Donated by Guna Kinne in 1989.
87. Holden prototype no. 1, 1946. Purchased in 2004.
88. John Moriarty's basket, about 1950. Purchased in 2009.
91. Propert caravan, 1956. Purchased in 1985.
92. Arthur Stewart's gold nugget, 1957. Purchased in 2011.
95. John Konrads' medal, 1960. Purchased in 2011.
96. Arthur Stace's Eternity sign, 1960s. Purchased in 2000.
99. Faith Bandler's gloves, 1960s. Donated by Faith Bandler in 1998.
101. Jack Wherra's boab nut, 1960s. Purchased in 2003.
102. Aurukun wallaby sculpture, 1962. Purchased in the 1970s.
104. Yirrkala bark petition, 1963. Donated by Gordon Bryant's family in 2009.
107. Mathaman Marika's bark painting, 1964. Transferred from Australian Institute of Aboriginal Studies Collection in 1984.
108. Narritjin Maymuru's creation story, about 1965. Transferred from Australian Institute of Anatomy Collection in 1984.
111. Expo Mark II sound chair, 1967. Purchased in 2007.
112. *Play School* rocket clock, 1976. Donated by the Australian Broadcasting Commission in 2006.
115. Azaria Chamberlain's black dress, 1980. Acquired in 2002.
116. Uta Uta Tjangala's painting, 1981. Transferred from the Aboriginal Arts Board in 1990.
119. *Đàn Tre*, 1981. Donated by Minh Tam Nguyen in 1990.
120. Peace bus, 1984. Donated by the People for Nuclear Disarmament in 1987.
123. *Harvest of Endurance* scroll, 1988. Purchased in 1992.
125. CSIRO WLAN test-bed, 1990s. Donated by CSIRO in 2011.
126. Ron Muncaster's platform shoe, 1994. Donated by Ron Muncaster in 2005.
128. *Ngurrara I*, 1996. Purchased in 2010.
131. Ken Thaiday's triple *beizam* headdress, 1999. Purchased in 2010.
132. Tristan Young's bush toys, 1999. Purchased in 2001.
135. Australian flag from the World Trade Center, 2001. Donated by the New York Police Department in 2004.
136. Dulcie Greeno's necklace, 2003. Purchased in 2003.
138. Esme Timbery's shellwork, 2006. Purchased in 2007.

© National Museum of Australia Press 2012

This book is copyright. Apart from any fair dealing for the purpose of private study, research, criticism or review as permitted under the *Copyright Act 1968* and subsequent amendments, no part of this publication may be reproduced, stored in a retrieval system, or transmitted in any form or by any means, electronic, mechanical, photocopying, recording or otherwise without prior written permission. Enquiries are to be made to the National Museum of Australia.

Every attempt has been made to contact artists and copyright holders for permission to reproduce their work in this book. Enquiries are to be made to the National Museum of Australia.

First published 2012 by
National Museum of Australia Press
GPO Box 1901
Canberra ACT 2601
Phone +61 2 6208 5000
Fax +61 2 6208 5148
www.nma.gov.au

National Library of Australia cataloguing-in-publication data
Collection stories / National Museum of Australia.

ISBN 9781921953132 (pbk.)

National Museum of Australia.
Museum exhibits — Australian Capital Territory — Canberra — Anecdotes.
National museums — Australian Capital Territory — Canberra — Anecdotes.
Exhibitions — Australian Capital Territory — Canberra — Anecdotes.
069.09947

Publications manager: Julie Ogden
Publisher's editor: Meredith McKendry, Therese Osborne

Contributors: Jay Arthur, Laura Breen, Ian Coates, Anne-Marie Condé, Carol Cooper, Alisa Duff, Sharon Goddard, Andy Greenslade, Anthea Gunn, Guy Hansen, Michelle Hetherington, Judith Hickson, Sophie Jensen, David Kaus, George Main, Stephen Munro, Daniel Oakman, Martha Sear, Peter Thorley, Jennifer Wilson

Design and typesetting: Po Sung
Copyright and image delivery: Denis French
Object photography: George Serras, Jason McCarthy, Dragi Markovic, Dean McNicoll, Lannon Harley
All archival photographs from National Museum of Australia, unless otherwise credited
Print: Imago

Cover image: Citroën 5CV with original licence plates and 1975 paintwork, 1923